THOUGHTS ON HIGHER EDUCATION IN INDIA

THOUGHTS ON HIGHER EDUCATION IN INDIA

A.S. Rao
and
P. Tauro

KALPAZ

ISBN: 978-93-5128-107-8

Price: ₹ 425

First Published 2015

Published by

Kalpaz Publications
C-30, Satyawati Nagar,
Delhi - 110052
E-mail: kalpaz@hotmail.com Ph.: 9212142040

Laser Typesetting : Rajender Vashist, Delhi
Printed at : G. Print Process, Delhi

Cataloging in Publication Data—DK
Courtesy: D.K. Agencies (P) Ltd. <docinfo@dkagencies.com>

Rao, A. S., author.
Thoughts on higher education in India / A.S. Rao and P. Tauro.
pages cm
Includes bibliographical references and index.
ISBN 9789351281078

1. Education, Higher—India. 2. Education, Higher—India—Societies, etc. 3. Higher education and state—India. I. Tauro, P., author. II. Title.

DDC 378.54 23

Contents

Foreword

This publication "Thoughts on higher education in India" includes a collection of commentaries written mostly by the first author Dr A.S. Rao and published in current science, Bengaluru and, university today, New Delhi. They include commentaries on the state of affairs in Higher University education in India. The articles expose most of the tribulations that plague our higher education system at the administrative and academic levels. In the past, the governments have attempted to improve higher education through various approaches including the constitution of various commissions. Sad as it may sound, not much improvement has happened as the reports are all shelved.

We have a number of institutions of higher learning in India of repute but unfortunately, politics get mixed with evil intentions in most and nothing is achieved. The committees and commissions set up by earlier governments made some very useful suggestions. No doubt, no one solution can suit all regions of our country but the commission's rfecommendations should have been discussed by the academics thoroughly and a more comprehensive plan to improve our higher education institutions should have emerged. Alas, this has not occurred. The UPA has now given place to NDA government and those interested in higher education are hoping for a change. With the change in the government, it appears that the policy makers at the top have decided to formulate a new policy. Today, we live in a globalised world and our institutions and students must meet global standards. There is therefore an urgent need to change the path of reform from the top and this needs knowledgeable policy makers at the top and good administrators to translate the policies.

The ruling NDA government has decided to open up a number of new institutions of higher education such as IIM, IITs, and others, despite knowing well that the existing ones are suffering from want of vision, funds, educated faculty and administration. Instead of first strengthening the existing universities and other institutions of higher learning, new institutions are donated to various states based on political considerations.

In such scenario, not much can be expected to change. The articles in this book highlight the authors' experience of more than three decades in different institutes in India and abroad. The authors' opinions expressed are based on the field situation prevailing in higher educational institutions in India and abroad. It is hoped the articles would be useful to all academicians, apex educational bodies and ministries of education both at central and state level. The first thing that must be attempted is to get rid of politics from institutions of higher learning. This is easier said than done. Merit should be basis of staff recruitment from the vice-chancellors downwards. A rigorous attempt is needed to analyse our higher education system vis a vis those that in some western countries. We should see what is best and what can be adapted to our conditions. Only then, our institutions may rise and compete with the best in the world.

These ideas presented herein have already been scrutinized and widely acknowledged by the academic community.

I wish the authors venture a grand success.

Dec. 2014

Dr M.V. Rao
Honorary Professor,
Department of Plant Sciences
Bharathidasan University,
Tiruchirappalli-620024
Tamil Nadu (India)

Acknowledgements

We wish to place on record our sincere thanks to Dr M.V. Rao, Honorary Professor, Department of Plant Sciences, Bharathidasan University, Tiruchirappalli-620024 for writing foreword for our book and to Mr R.G. Bharadwaj and Mr Parthibhjan Research scholars for assisting in the computer work.

A.S. Rao
P. Tauro

Introduction

The Indian higher education system is the largest in the world next only to the USA and China. It is governed by the University Grants Commission (UGC) which functions under the Ministry of Human Resources Development. The UGC is expected to set up standards, enforce them and help to coordinate between the centre and state governments in implementing its suggestions. Accreditation of universities which meet the standards is the responsibility of the UGC. Unfortunately, the UGC functions as a unit of the political party in power. Accreditation committees as well as evaluation committees malfunction with the result that their recommendations generally land in a court of law. Although the UGC can advise, it is not mandatory for the states to take the advise and as a result, it remains primarily an advisory body of the central government.

In recent years, the Indian higher education system has expanded in both the private and public sectors. Today in this globalised world, we need universities that meet global standards and produces students that are acceptable to the entire globe. Although students from some institutions are accepted all around the world, the majority are unemployable. This is mainly because Universities have mushroomed all over the country, not with the intention of imparting better education to our youngsters but primarily with the objective of making money. Quality is the last item on the mind of those who are setting up Universities using political clout and unaccounted money. No wonder, therefore, India does not have a university which can be ranked in the top one hundred in the world.

Higher education is a complex subject. It needs knowledgeabale policy makers who lay down new policies consistent with new developments. It needs an efficient, honest and non-corrupt administration that executes the laid down policies. Unfortunately this has not happened as we frequently hear about the poor policy decisions made by the politically appointed heads. The Universities also need dedicated teachers who are good at delivery. Nothing can substitute the human interaction in teaching and discussion that good teachers cultivate in the classrooms. The students also cannot escape their responsibility. Higher education system need students who are responsible for their education. Sad it may sound, all these things are at a minimum in Indian universities.

The government has from time to time constituted various committees such as Kothari commission, Yashpal committee, etc to advise on improving higher education. The UPA government had constituted National Knowledge Commission to improve higher education. The recommendations made by these committees have received little academic evaluation. The UPA government had also planned to introduce a new act to establish a National Commission for Higher Education and Research (NCHER) to bring in a new set of legislation to reform our higher education system. The act also envisaged to bring in autonomy in higher education so that search for knowledge and innovation is unhindered. The act had plans to bring in reforms in the regulatory process and improve the governing of our institutions by improving the manner in which the head of the institutions are chosen. A reform agenda for the faculty, students, public and the administrators was envisaged. The UPA II had also announced a *Rashtriya Uchchat Shikshan Abhiya* (RUSA) to strengthen higher education in India.

The problem in Indian universities begins from the top. The UGC is the main regulatory agency under the ministry of HRD. It has the responsibility of framing guidelines for efficient functioning of the universities. Unfortunately, in recent years, it has only become an arm of the government. The recent case is the Delhi University's four years undergraduate programme which was introduced at the behest of the previous government through the UGC. The very institution which had supported this programme a year ago, ensured that it was abandoned without any discussion.

The less said is better about the recruitment of the heads of our institutions. Vice-chancellors of universities are selected not on academic and administrative merit but on proximity to the politicians. Political support and ability to pay and buy, have been the root causes. Vice chancellors who have administrative and academic abilities are not wanted since they generally do not listen to their political masters. Hence with the top being rotten, one cannot expect better things down the line. Selection of faculty in universities is no better. It is manipulated based on caste rather than on merit. An institution of higher learning which does not have a talented faculty cannot attract talented students and the product is bound to be mediocre. One cannot expect much from the faculty which has not been selected based on talent and this is a major cause of the poor scientific output. Ethics have lost place in our higher education system and today plagiarism has become rampant. With publishers by the roadside with no ability to judge the good from the bad in science is a major cause of poor output by the university faculty. Although there is software to catch those who plagiarise few bother to use it. Overcrowding with students, improper guidance in writing assignments and theses and the lack of adequate competence in the English language, are some of the reasons that force the students to plagiarise.

There is also talk about bringing in foreign universities to open up shops in India primarily to help our universities to improve by copying the foreign element and also prevent Indian students from going abroad. Eminent personalities such as Mr Narayana Murthy have advocated this. Sad as it may sound, no good university from abroad will open shop in India without being able to make money which can be taken back to support their institutions in their countries. Secondly, a majority of students who go abroad for undergraduate and post-graduate education do so with the intention of staying there. Unless the universities which open shop in India guarantee the students an entry into their countries after graduation, no student will venture to get into these foreign universities in India. Small countries such as a Singapore and Dubai have attracted top universities and institutions from the west to establish their centres but India has not been able to do this mainly because of the fear of the government interference and retrospective laws.

In such scenario, not much can be expected to change. This book comprising of policy articles is based on the authors experience of more than three decades in different institutes in India and abroad. The authors opinions expressed are based on the field situation prevailing in higher educational institutions. Going through the articles one will understand as what ails our higher education. The first thing that must be attempted is to get rid of politics from Universities and other institutions of higher education.

Unfortunately, politicians believe that without their involvement, the institutions cannot run. Merit should be basis of staff recruitment from the vice-chancellors downwards. A rigorous attempt should be made to analyse our higher education system vis a vis as those that exist in some western countries. We should see what is best and what can be adapted to our conditions. Only then, our institutions may rise and compete with the best in the world.

Feedback on the opinions expressed is welcome at adhikaria@gmail.com

A.S. Rao

P. Tauro

A. Indian Universities, UGC, NKC, RUSA

1
An Ambience to Perform Well

A.S. Rao

Plagiarism and misconduct (P and M) has become a topical subject in India. One can analyse this and suggest remedial measures1-3, or just ignore it as there are sufficient number of persons who do not indulge in P and M, or look at it as a serious problem that could assume dangerous proportions if ignored.

P and M is possible at all levels and by all categories of academicians. One of the root causes of this problem is that the gargantuan expansion in education has not been met with the required increase in grants and expert faculty. Till this shortage is overcome, apex bodies could bring about certain reforms to minimise P and M.

One such reform could be to abolish mandatory project work at the under-graduate, postgraduate and M Phil levels, considering the enormous number of students. This slot could be substituted with an alternative programme — for example, many students are interested in clearing NET/SLET exams (for joining national institutes for a Ph.D), GRE (both general and subject), TOEFL/ IELTS (English language exams) or preparing for different jobs.

Another change could be to decide on the number of Ph.D students that a faculty member can guide based on the grants and facilities available with him/ his institute. Any kind of excessive pressure on students and faculty to perform may create a stressful situation, which can be contagious and compromise value judgements.

Many Indian students go abroad and perform commendably, clearly indicating their potential capabilities. What we need to do is to create an ambience for them to perform well in our country.

References

1. Satija, M. P., Univ. News, 2011, 49, 4-8.
2. Desai, P. N., *The New Indian Express*, Chennai, 15th October 2011, p. 8.
3. Rajput, J. S., *The New Indian Express*, Chennai, 16th October 2011, p. 9.

Published: *Current Science*, Vol. 102, No. 5, 10 March 2012.

2

Why No Indian University in World's Top 200?

A.S. Rao and *P. Tauro*

In our opinion following are some of the reasons:

(IIT's, IIM's, research institutes etc. cannot be categorised as regular universities. Hence, even if they figure under top 200 they should not be taken into consideration. Hence, only regular universities have been taken into consideration for giving the rankings).

It is an annually recurring topic for discussion as to why no Indian university figures in the top? Whatever may be the reasons it is impossible for any of our university to figure in the top overnight or in the near future. It is a time taking process. If we start today we may make it up after sometime.

1. At the outset I must say that teaching is a thankless job in our country. Hypocritically lot of hue and cry is made about severe shortage of teachers, particularly experienced ones. It is always research parameters that are considered for any promotion, recognition etc. Teaching and Teachers are relegated to the minimum possible vis-a-vis their research counter parts with the result researchers both genuine and so called neglect classes either in letter orin spirit, because it does not interfere in no way with their career prospects. Teacher absenteeism is very high in India. As long teaching

and teachers are neglected no university can become a world class and we will continue to be at the bottom of the world university ranking list.

2. Recruitment in the departments is highly ill planned and therefore departments consists of a randomly assorted faculty. Often there are inadequate faculty keeping in view the nature of the subject.
3. No rigid degree qualifications requirement and screening for recruitment to a post. After doing an UG, the candidate can do PG in any Dept., Ph.D in any Dept. and job in yet another Dept. In USA such things may happen but with rigorous remedial course work.
4. Indiscriminate starting of course programmes and intake of students without any regard for the availability of infrastructure, funds and manpower to train the students.
5. Being a country with high population universities have mushroomed (and still there is a demand for huge number of universities). Correspondingly we do not have good teachers, researchers and funds to train the students.
6. Highly interrupted power and water supply, a problem persistent since decades.
7. Funding agencies do not fund till the end of the goal and by western standards the funding is inadequate. They also cannot fund faculty in all the 543 degree awarding institutes till the end of the career. It will be a chequered career for most and teaching does not fetch.
8. A research worker simultaneously works on different goals (each Ph.D student works on a different goal) and finally no goal is achieved.The way UN identifies MDG (Millennium Development Goals) we do not identify our research goals and accordingly fund. Hence, lot of money is wasted in carrying out routine confirmatory research to roll out more number of Ph.D's for survival.
9. Administrative responsibilities, attending to various

conferences, symposia etc. and various forms of outsourcing and more number of holidays is leading to meagre attention to Ph.D students and classes.

10. Foundation of students is very weak because of inadequate training in schools and colleges.

Published: University Today, 2013, 33(9) 8.

3

What should be the Difference(s) between a College, University and a Research Institute?

A.S. Rao

I feel a debate/discussion is warranted on 'What should be the difference(s) between a college, university and a research institute so that these three levels of educational institutes can rightly evolve and cater to the needs of the society/nation in the new millennium.

The country should first come to a consensus as to how many universities and colleges it should have for a population of one billion plus. How many students should each university and college have? What should be the different programmes? Should these programmes be identical or different between a college and a university? How many students should be brought into each programme? In what manner should a programme be run? (For example, an M.Sc. programme may be run with or without a dissertation; a Ph.D programme may be run with or without a course programme, etc. How should the teacher-student ratio vary in a college and a university? Should colleges continue to be affiliated to universities? If not, who should regulate their functioning? If yes, to what extent should colleges abide by the universities? Can a teacher with M.Sc./MA qualification teach M.Sc./MA students or do you expect the teacher to possess a Ph.D to teach them?

Once upon a time colleges were meant only for undergraduate (UG) programmes and universities for postgraduate (PG) programmes and Ph.D/DSc research. The faculty in the research institutes were exclusively devoted to research by themselves (i.e. without the help of any Ph.D students). A while later, colleges started a few programmes and some universities started a few special UG programmes. Of late some are of the opinion that universities also should start their own UG programmes as they are likely to be of a higher quality than that of colleges. Is this going to happen?

Now we have colleges roiling out a very large number of PG students than universities. More and more colleges are likely to follow this trend. Colleges run many PG programmes which a university normally runs. Faculty in colleges also register Ph.D students and apply for research projects. (And this tendency is likely to increase.) In some places, the teaching load of university faculty is similar to colleges or even more. On the other extreme we also have some non-teaching departments in on universities, i.e., which do not run any UG/PG programmes but register only Ph.D students. Many faculty in the university have no research funding for most of their career. We have research institutes regularly taking varying number of Ph.D students and some participate in teaching programmes also, at M.Sc./Ph.D level. More and more research institutes are becoming eager to undertake Ph.D students. Further, once someone made a recommendation that all the research institutes (particular reputed ones) should start their own M.Sc. programmes in different disciplines as they are likely to be of a higher quality than that of colleges. Is this going to happen (All these may be advantageous to students but is tantamount to serious deprivation of the universities of funds, good students and good working hands.)

Published: *Current Science*, Vol. 78, No, 2525 January 2000 119.

4

Latest UGC Regulations: Dissected

A.S. Rao and *P. Tauro*

Introduction

University Grants Commission released its latest regulations in the September issue of 2010. They deal with the minimum qualifications for the appointment of teachers and other academic staff in universities and colleges. They also deal with measures for the maintenance of standards in higher education. It is not clear as to the values cherished based on which the bars of standards could be fixed. Even after 14 months, whether or not all state governments expressed their agreeability and begin to implement. Therefore, a perusal of issues, albeit belated, is in order.

1. What is mandatory and what are just guide lines?

Higher education being a concurrent subject it is a matter of speculation as to how much of the revised regulations (1) are binding on the state. As rightly suggested by the TNGCTA (Tamil Nadu Government College Teachers Association) "pay scales, retirement age, promotion policies, recruitment qualifications .... pension rules" are fundamental principles and need to be followed (by states as well) as per UGC norms (2). Further, faculty in the state universities avail lesser perks (Regulation 11.0). Faculty in state institutions should not be demoralised because of the wide differences with their counterparts in the centre in the benefits. UGC should take cognizance of this view which is strongly expressed and documented (3) and in fact 150VC's have resolved in Delhi about the retirement age being 65. Even then it is not implemented.

From the past experience one may say that each state may take its own time to implement and have its own way of implementing the regulations not only in the above parameters but also other parameters. It is a must that UGC pin points what is mandatory and what is just a guide line? If nothing is or fundamental principles are not mandatory then better move the subject from concurrent list to state list. Atleast state will ensure uniformity among all its universities. Of course, personally we feel as education and science and technology is vital for the development of the society and the country higher education subject should be entirely with the centre. Atleast the universities may be under centre and the colleges be under the respective state directorate of collegiate education.

2. Can UGC monitor implementation nationwide?

Is it possible for the UGC to monitor the vast number of colleges and universities whether its various regulations are being followed or not? Does it have any mechanism to identify the institutes for any omissions which can be different in different states and in different universities within a state?

3. How much legal are the regulations?

It is better if the regulations are scrutinised by an eminent panel of lawyers and take their opinion for any loop holes or subjectivity in interpreting the regulations. Accordingly they may be modified. Only then UGC can ensure that the regulations are not interpreted differently by different states and different universities within a state. Such an opinion of differential interpretation has been there since long. Further, what often a university follows is a random combination of rules of the UGC, State Gov., decisions of other universities and its own syndicate. Thus, a university can frame a chimeric set of rules for policy formulation. Autonomy should not mean that each university functions in a different way. British officers in their interest often used to make an exception and approve a case noting on the file." This shall not be quoted as a precedence". And this was respected by the subsequent officers. Now in independent India this is not possible and without any big discussion quoting a precedence-however undesirable it is-and approving a case is not uncommon. Possessing a data base of all bad precedents is an asset to an administrator and faculty alike.

4. Technical programmes need to be under technical apex bodies

When once the concept of specific professional universities has been approved by the Government i.e., universities of medical, agriculture, engineering and technology etc. all the colleges in the erstwhile traditional universities should have been transferred to the respective professional universities and the power earlier vested in them to start professional colleges and programmes should have been scrapped simultaneously. This has not happened. Even today we find above colleges and professional programmes under traditional universities. That is, under the same roof and administration different sets of regulations are to be followed for different faculty. Why two parallel systems? If need be more professional universities may be started.

In case of engineering and technology colleges and programmes the situation is little more complicated as traditional universities need not take the approval of AICTE to start the same. These students may be discriminated over the students who have rolled out from AICTE approved institutions.

5. UGC role in the implementation of reservation system

Every state has its own communal reservation system. The number of categories and the proportion under each of these categories varies widely from state to state. To appease all the communal categories, for all designations and for all departments and at administration level as well, is an impossible task. UGC may ponder over this and give some instructions.

THE TRINNEAL TAMASHA

6. Pro-VC post should be the senior-most professor. Assessment of the outgoing VC should precede the appointment of his successor.

Pro-VC post is lacking in most universities. A circular in this regard be sent to all universities to fill up this post at the earliest. Does UGC specify any functions for this post or it is only to be delegated to by the VC? The Pro-VC post should be from the main university campus on the basis of seniority. This would avoid unnecessary manoeuvring. Alternatively, this post may be abolished.

7. Either the VC or Registrar should be an IAS officer

Comparing across the country, we had been having VC's from IAS and even state public service commissions. Even judges were recommended. Does UGC bar the above categories? There are still faculty who honestly feels that an efficient rule minded IAS officer is better rather an academician who comes with his own personal lobbies and prejudices. Ills plaguing can be different for different universities in the country like student unrest and law order, aggressive unions, divisive faculty, raising standards of the university, need for specific future tasks, administrative and financial problems, need for man power and infrastructure development, establishment of a new university etc. So often a VC needs to be selected and appointed keeping the needs and problems of the specific university in mind rather than treating all universities on par and call for a general selection process. Concerned State Government and Chancellor/visitor should first take up this exercise. A VC should be selected at least three months before the tenure of the earlier VC expires. In case of Registrar also IAS, state public service commission people and Deputy Registrars from Non-Teaching cadre (i.e. office staff) had been holding the post. Does UGC bar the above categories? Though UGC has mentioned selection criteria, prescribed qualifications, search committees etc. for all posts, there is no such mention anywhere in the gazette for Registrar Post. May be an inadvertent omission of this item

'Registrar'. While it is clear in case of a Deputy Controller of examination post, it is not clear whether an academician can be deputed to the post of Deputy Registrar. If so there should be at least one post filled from the university.

FACULTY-GUIDELINES

8. Terminology describing qualifications is highly subjective and will lead to malpractices

There can be a controversy in the terminology used while indicating the qualifications for recruitment (I did consult some English professors too in this regard). Concerned/relevant/ appropriate and in many other advertisements in the country the terms respective/ corresponding/specific/particular/major also are used. Further, in this multidisciplinary era the term "allied" also is controversial. Similarly with the terms, subject/branch/discipline. There is a scope for disagreement among and within the faculty, screening and selection committee members and job aspirants. To prevent abuse of the stipulations by indulging in hair splitting semantics and perverted arguments while recruitment, UGC may clarify the above terminology by preparing a suitable table taking into consideration the list of departments, degrees conferred and subjects in which NET. etc. is conducted. UGC can have access to all this information. The table may indicate the apt terminology as a caption in the columns. Normally in a university, Departments run programs and offer PG and Ph.D degrees bearing the name of the department. Such students may feel they have a 4 greater claim to join that department (Some departments in addition or exclusively may run programmes and offer degrees which do not tally with the name of the Department). Academic freedom and flexibility in mobility should not mean indiscriminate eligibility either for offering degrees or acquiring degrees or for claiming posts. State Universities and Governments may get tempted or otherwise compelled to imitate the serious malpractices pointed out by (5) not only in the contractual appointments but also of guest lecturers. UGC should take a serious note of this article.

9. Description and representation of GPA table is faulty

Description and representation of grade point table is faulty (Reg.5.0). Second column does not represent grade points. Range of values represent grade point average (GPA) that too only to assign an attribute like outstanding, good etc. Otherwise grade points and a GPA obtained by a candidate is a fixed value and candidates securing a certain range of marks, say 65-74 as in the table would have the same grade point average. That is to say a candidate who has secured 65 marks and another candidate who has secured 74 marks (i.e., nine marks more) both are given the same grade and will earn the same grade points. Since some institutes feel that nine marks range is a big difference, they choose a five mark range, say 61-65, 66-70 and so on. Here, also all candidates who have secured marks within the range will be placed in the same grade and will earn the same grade points. Because of this, in this era of severe competition students insist to indicate both marks and GPA in the transcript to further differentiate the candidates with the same GPA for any selection. UGC has represented a six-point system calling it as on the scale of seven. We have other point systems, 4, 5 ...10. Where the attributes given to the marks are different. In my opinion 55 per cent marks in a grade point system cannot be called as good but average or below average. Where traditional annual system is still being followed 55 per cent is fine. Further, 75-100 is too broad a range to group candidates together as mentioned by UGC. Alternatively stick only to letter grading and do not show any marks in the transcript if the variation of marks does not matter.

10. Sanctioned posts should not be cleared without government concurrence

The term "sanctioned post" by UGC is a sort of misnomer. Because, UGC pays the salary towards these posts only initially for a limited period of time. The university has to incur the burden for the remaining 20-30 years plus pension benefits for which it has to plead and pursue the state government. This is also the case with posts sanctioned by different funding agencies. The state government need not have any responsibility for this commitment as these posts are claimed and filled up without the written concurrence from the state Government in view of the autonomous status of a university. Therefore, a prior approval by the concerned State Government for any post sanctioned by UGC or any other external agencies must be there. Only then UGC etc. should release the posts. In view of the autonomous nature of the university they may appoint the faculty even if no agency or State Government sanctions them. Such autonomy is not desirable.

11. UGC prescribed work load contradicts ground realities

Work load and leave rules (15.0 and 8.4)-40 hours of full employment prescribed by UGC does not fit into the official timings of a large number of institutes. They may function from 35-39 hours. Taking the local example for the year 2011, without applying for any leave we get 170 holidays. That is, even if you do not take any leave there are only 97 days per semester which are not sufficient for teaching, exams and preparation. After availing the prescribed leaves in different categories only 117 working days are left i.e., approximately 60 days per semester. Attending official meetings and functions and seminars and Viva Voce of students, special lectures etc. further deprives the students of a teacher at least by another 10 days. It is simply not possible to have 180 teaching days plus another eight weeks for exams and preparation. (This data does not vary widely from year to year or across the country. Compensatory classes are difficult to arrange in view of so many holidays, and all faculty availing the leaves as above and less number of faculty in a department to handle all the topics in the required papers). Therefore, for effective teaching and training, the numbers of holidays in some categories have to be reduced. It is not just the claim of heads of the departments, even non-teaching staff would vouch for a minimum of two hours per day work for an HOD in any viable department. That amounts to at least 10 hours per week. Adding six hours for research recommended by UGC, it amounts to sixteen hours. Hence, HODs should have the freedom to be exempted from teaching responsibilities. While computing work load time involved in preparing the lectures have to be included. This can vary depending on the situation. A faculty with eight Ph.D students and projects is it not on a whole time job? Many responsibilities related to institutional governance mentioned by the UGC takes a lot of time and such faculty should be duly exempted from teaching responsibilities. UGC has not mentioned one important post concerning institutional governance i.e. member of the syndicate / Board of management. In the API scores they should be given at least 15 marks. In a university it is difficult to do due justice to more than two papers/semester of four credits each.

12. Judicious composition of a department

The UGC should strongly emphasise the need to plan the composition of a department. If majority of the faculty in a department belong to the same or overlapping interests such departments are highly deficient. A department should have faculty with clear cut differences in fields of specialisations relevant to the teaching programs and thrust areas of research. Existing sister departments also may be kept in mind in this regard. UGC may also give some regulations and suggestions regarding the starting of new departments and programs in a university. Further,UGC should give guidelines to assess the viability of a department or a program and to accordingly take steps. For example, there is no point in running programs with a skeleton strength.

13. Appointments should be the best from all over the country

Even with the present number of colleges and universities if there is a severe shortage of faculty in many disciplines, how the policy makers and various associations are demanding further heavy expansion? How they are expecting to increase the gross enrolment ratio still further? Further, Ph.D qualification has been made dispensable even at Associate and Professor levels. In the absence of UGC giving any reasons, we have to presume that there is a severe shortage of Ph.Ds in these fields. When there is a crisis there is nothing wrong if we attract people with desired qualifications from all over the globe rather than to run our programmes appointing persons with compromised qualifications.

API SCORES

14. Building API scores fast hinders proper execution of academic activities

Everyone wants to rise and achieve the required API scores in as short time as possible. This can lead to a serious compromise in the execution of various activities mentioned in Categories I, II and III in Appendix III.

15. Computing API scores for academicians deputed to administrative posts

For faculty deputed to whole time administrative jobs like Registrar, Controller of examinations, Deputy Controller etc. for that period Category I evaluation cannot be made (Teaching, learning and evaluation related activities). To some extent problem may be there in Category II and III. Similar problem may be there for persons coming from research and industrial organisations. For computing API scores for the above categories of people UGC may give some additional instructions.

16. Computation of API scores and interviews on the same day: Incorrect

Computation of API scores and Interviews cannot be done on the same day as suggested by UGC, as many candidates may apply for a post. The screening committee has to do the API calculations much before the interview letters are sent. Since interview carries only 20 per cent weightage the remaining 80 per cent is known much before the interview! Another question that arises is on what basis to decide how many and whom to call for interview?

OTHER RULES

17. Revision of rules for appointment of Associate Professor and direct recruitment as Professor

Rule 3.8.0 Gives an impression that Ph.D is not required for promotion as associate professor through CAS (Career Advancement Scheme). Ph.D should be made mandatory even through CAS. For any higher post a certain minimum length of service in the immediate preceding cadre should be made mandatory. No such recommendation is given for Professor Post though a long period of eight years as assistant professor has been made mandatory to become an associate professor. A minimum of five years of associate experience must be there for a Professor post under direct recruitment which should be still more in case of CAS and not just three years as mentioned in Rule 6.4.8. The reg. 4.1.0 B wherein outstanding candidates can be accommodated is very vital and therefore should not be so cryptic and general. It should be considerably elaborated to assist in the objective assessment of outstanding candidates.

18. Sabbatical with pay and allowances for Assistant Professors

It is very unfair not to grant sabbatical leave for Assistant Professors. They are younger and are likely to be more efficient at bench work. In fact many foreign Post Doc advertisements mention, that only those candidates not latter that three-five years after obtaining Ph.D may apply for positions. Rule 8.3 V is not teacher friendly and gives scope for arbitrariness. The faculty granted sabbatical leave should avail full pay and allowances in all circumstances and should not be discretionary.

19. HOD rotation down to the level of Assistant Professor

There is no mention either of tenure and / or selection criteria for many administrative posts like principal, head of the departments, Deans, chairs etc. it is strange that though rotation of head of the departments has started operating in this country since 1983, there are still universities which do not implement the rotation policy. This shows how helpless UGC is in not able to ensure uniformity in the in the implementation of fundamental principles. Further, we feel that HOD rotation should be done down to the level of Assistant professors. When assistant professors are holding the HOD post as regular HOD's what is the hitch in making them as HOD for a limited period of time under rotation policy? One of my teachers used to say that when he was in USA he had witnessed departments with eminent professors and even Nobel laureates being headed by just an assistant professor. Even today you may have such a situation in USA. HOD post should be made such that it is an additional responsibility and service to the department and not as a post to further their interests by all means and trouble the subordinates, research scholars and students and play politics in the university. Rotation down to the level of assistant professors drastically mitigates the above problems.

20. For all promotions, a minimum service in the preceding cadre mandatory

Counting of past services is another controversial issue. It is a matter of common knowledge that in private institutes positions are purely temporary and the salary structure, selection of candidates, conditions of appointment and conferring designations is the privilege of the promoters. It is very difficult to ascertain the facts which UGC recommends under clause 10.1 nor is it possible for the private institutions to run their programmes as per the conditions in the above clause. Hence, there are a large number of candidates who want to leave private institutesand join Government institutes. State Government takes into consideration the past experience only to select candidates at the entry level as Assistant Professor. The past experience before joining the Government service does not figure for any subsequent promotions. Their subsequent promotions are entirely based on the length of the services rendered in the Government service. This is the right procedure. Similar procedure should be followed in universities too. For candidates who wish to join universities from Government organisations for higher posts of Associate professor and Professor,

UGC should insist on a certain minimum length of service in the immediate preceding cadre to be eligible for direct recruitment.

21. A Ph.D for librarian post and retirement age on par with others

4.5.1- For a university librarian post which is of a Professor scale, not only Ph.D even M.Phil. has been made only as a desirable qualification but they have to spend 13 years as deputy librarian in a university or 18 years in a college. In case the candidate possesses Ph.D the above length of service may be lowered. UGC also says that there is no shortage of candidates in Library science. Combining both the statements it appears, there are too many candidates in library science without Ph.D What efforts UGC is taking to overcome the shortage of Ph.Ds not only in library science but also in other fields except increasing the retirement age of the existing people? Paradoxically UGC says there is no increase in the retirement age for librarians.

DOCTORAL STUDENTS

22. Compulsory in-house training for all categories of Doctoral students

UGC has rightly decided that the time taken to acquire Ph.D degree shall not be considered as experience to be claimed for appointments. But UGC did not consider the fact that faculty can acquire Ph.D without spending anytime! Faculty can register for and complete the Ph.D remaining in service and Hence, they are simultaneously getting both Ph.D and counting the time towards experience. This trend is likely to continue in a large way as there are a large number of candidates without Ph.D both in government and private institutions. Those who do Ph.D in a regular mode can be at a disadvantage vis-a-vis those who do Ph.D as above. Hence, UGC should curb the above practice and make it mandatory for every faculty to take leave and then do Ph.D with a minimum residential requirement of three years. Even this is less to roll out a good Ph.D which may take four-five years as in reputed institutes. However, in view of API scores to be realised early the duration of Ph.D may be compromised by the supervisors. The policy of UGC to give a onetime grant for those who have rolled out 15 Ph.D's is another incentive to compromise the duration of in-house training. Alternatively UGC should distinguish between pre-doctoral and post-doctoral length of service and insist on certain minimum length of service after acquiring Ph.D for the faculty who do Ph.D as above (i.e. without taking leave) for considering them for direct recruitment or CAS promotions. Many PG degrees, M.Sc, M.Phil. and M.Tech. and other degrees may be obtained by alternative modes of education without any loss to experience. The more important point for UGC to consider here is, should there not be any restriction on the disciplines in which degrees can be obtained through alternative modes of education

23. Dispensability of NET and separate tests in life sciences

NET etc has been exempted for all disciplines in engineering and technology (except for Biotech-eng and tech stream. Reason is not clear. (Infect many engineering colleges still assert that it is not required even for M.Tech-Biotech students) If AICTE and other professional bodies can do away with entrance test for their respective teaching profession UGC also may do away with the entrance test. For gaining fellowships entrance test is fine. More over NET etc. is not available in all subjects and UGC has exempted in such cases. Even in subjects in which it is available, the candidates with pass in NET etc. are inadequate to cater to the needs of the huge expansion in education. Suppose private colleges make a request to the university that they may be allowed to appoint candidates without NET etc. as no candidate with NET etc. has responded to their advertisement, can their programs be stopped ? It has been a practice to approve all such cases and such approvals will have to continue. This happens in Government institutions also in case of subjects where NET etc. is not conducted. A university or even a Government college may start such programs where NET etc. is not available. It is common to start new programs every year by colleges and universities in which NET etc. is not available. There is a genuine grouse among students of different life science subjects. They are a large number.

In these days when specialisation of subjects like microbiology, biochemistry, biotechnology etc. are available even at UG level, there are many who do both UG and PG in the above subjects. They honestly feel, they have a greater chance to clear the exam if NET etc. is conducted specifically in the above subjects based on their syllabus rather than a common test for all life science students. Even those who do only their PG in the above subjects feel so Microbiology and biochemistry are age old departments and Biotech though 25 years old its expansion has been tremendous as with microbiology and biochemistry departments. When the number of students getting rolled out with PG degrees in the above subjects are so high, it is only fair that separate tests are conducted in the above subjects. Similar grouse may be there for students in other subjects. (DBT gives a limited number of fellowships in biotech and bioinformatics). Ideal options are (a) not to have test for any subject or (b) conduct tests for all subjects and discourage running of programmes for which UGC is not able to conduct a test.

POINTS TO PONDER

24. UGC regulations should mandate a NAAC assessment

A copy of UGC regulations should be given to NAAC committee accrediting every institute. NAAC assessment should have considerable weightage for the UGC regulations. NAAC committee as a priority should evaluate to what extent an institute is following UGC regulations and recommendations. This component should be given a good scoring. UGC may even suggest that if certain recommendations—which UGC feels as very important- are not followed—the accreditation maybe deferred till they are implemented. This makes the concerned state governments. more responsible towards UGC recommendations and also in monitoring the affairs of the universities.

25. Administrative reforms, supporting services and revision of acts and statutes are natural corollaries

UGC has given these regulations for maintenance of standards in higher education. It is equally important that UGC also frames regulations leading to administrative reforms and accordingly amendment of acts and statutes of the universities. Lot of problems and friction may be minimised by bringing suitable administrative reforms.The concept of supporting services for research and teaching is lacking. UGC should recommend recruitment of some number of technicians and lab attenders to assist in conducting practicals and research and secretarial assistance.

26. Can or will all faculties grow?

While it is to be appreciated to insist the faculty to maintain certain level of API (Academic Performance Indicator) scores, it is only fair that the system should provide ample and equal opportunities to all to perform. Is this possible for such a large number of faculty in the country? API scores in Category III (Research and academic contributions) is totally linked to obtaining grants and the intake and demand for M.Phil and Ph.D. students. All these may different widely from university to university. It may not be possible to fund all the faculty in all the universities to any appreciable extent nor there an adequate intake and demand for M.Phil. and Ph.D students everywhere, but all faculty wants to grow as fast as possible. Decline of funding even to central universities because of diversion of funds to national institutes, is a disturbing fact (3,4). Funding for state universities is still less as compared to central universities. To ease the situation UGC may help the universities to establish a good central instrumentation facility duly manned and a certain amount of annual grant be given to every faculty for recurring expenditure. Keeping so many variations and constraints across the country there may be a relaxation in the total API scores required under Category III.

27. Are the present UGC rules adequate to transform our universities into world class?

Every year we get embarrassed knowing that not even a single Indian university figures in the top 100-200 in the world depending on the ranking organisation and even among the top 500 very few are there. (Except for Calcutta university others are IIT's and IISC which are not regular universities) (6-8). Does UGC has any plans to frame a separate set of regulations to transform any or some of the existing universities into world class universities? Or the present regulations are sufficient? It is depressing to note that often big shots talk about making IITs, IIMs etc. (which are not regular universities) as world class institutes but do not talk about regular universities achieving global excellence. What is the relevance of hundreds of regular universities if they are not considered for up gradation into world class universities?

Acknowledgements

I sincerely thank many colleagues and students for deliberations, in particular Dr P. Sudhakar Swamy Professor and Head, Dept. Plant sciences, Madurai Kamraj university, Madurai and Dr. M.V. Rao, Professor and Head Dept. Plant Science Bharathidasan University, Tiruchirappalli.

References

1. UGC regulations on minimum qualifications for appointment of teachers and other academic staff in universities and colleges and measures for the maintenance of standards III Sec 4, pp. 7848-7996. In higher education 2010. The Gazette of India, 2010 September 18, part III.
2. The Hindu, 2011, Tiruchirappalli edition, p. 2.
3. Deepak Kumar., Curr.Sci. 2011, 101,149. 4.
4. Mitra, A.N., Curr. Sci. 2011, 101, 716.
5. Anil Singh., Curr. Sci. 101,716.
6. Balaram, P., Curr.Sci. 2011, 100, 1601-1602.
7. 2011 World University Web ranking-www.4icu.org/top200/
8. articles.timesofindia.com/2010-19-17.

Published: University Today, 2012, 32(1) 6-8.

5

UGC Model Curriculum: Some Suggestions for the Next Edition

A.S. Rao

The University Grants Commission (UGC) has recently circulated model curricula for 33 subjects. I have some comments on the post-graduate programs.

- First of all, the size of the curriculum is different in different subjects, running to as little as 30 pages in some subjects to more than 500 pages in some others. This is because different committees have discussed altogether different details and/or the same details to different depths. Each committee has evolved its own format of presentation of details and there has been no proof reading.
- There is no uniformity in the terminology, abbreviations and captions used by different committees while presenting the details of the curriculum.
- Total number of papers and credits recommended is different for different subjects. Hence, the credit/work load and the total number of marks for a two-year postgraduate programme are different in different subjects. Weightage given to theory vis-a-vis laboratory and compulsory vis-a-vis optional courses is considerably different.

Further, the scheduling of recommended courses over the semesters like compulsory topics/electives, etc. is also different. Not all universities in the country insist on project work. Even in the same university, some colleges complete the degree with project work and some without it. This makes sense. There are lot of practical difficulties and undesirable consequences, if project work is made obligatory in view of the huge number of students involved.

- Though UGC recommends choice-based credit system, the system to be adopted has not been apparently appraised to the committees. It is probably not in the spirit of the credit system to have as many theory and laboratory courses as suggested in different programmes. Credit system demands that there be a shift in the pattern of examination and evaluation. UGC has not dwelt on this.
- There should not be any ambiguity in the 'formal instructional time' prescribed. Unfortunately, there is too much of flexibility now; the number of days per semester varies anywhere from 60 to 90 days per semester. Committees should also ponder over the question, 'How much time is really required to cover the recommended syllabus to the desired depth, both from the teacher's and student's point of view?'
- UGC does not mention anything about course work for Ph.D programmes. Students come from a variety of backgrounds to register for Ph.D in the same discipline.
- The extent to which bibliography is given, as also its manner and format vary a lot between and within a curriculum. Moreover, there are no electronic references in any curriculum, which are must nowadays and are given in modern textbooks.
- Mentioning clearly the requirements of human, financial and material sources for running a specific programme may help the relevant authorities to take steps, to ensure some standards.
- The manner in which course contents of the syllabus are introduced is different. For example, while some directly start listing the contents, others give a caption like learning outcome, course rationale, etc. The way the syllabus is further divided also is different.

Published: *Current Science*, Vol. 85, No. 7, 10 October 2003

6

Additional Recommendations to the UGC Task Force for Basic Scientific Research in Universities

A.S. Rao

Recently, an article appeared in *The New Indian Express* (1). Highlighting the decreased enrolment in basic sciences and listing out a ten point recommendation by the UGC task force to attract and train students. A professional treatment of the subject is given by Balaram (2,3). I wish to suggest a few additional points which may be necessary not only to basic sciences but also to other programmes.

(a) Money should be provided for inviting subject experts from far and near, with provision for air travel and local hospitality, Four to six experts may be needed every semester, for adequate interaction with students.

(b) Efforts must be made to organise video conferencing with eminent scientists.

(c) Practical training is a causality for lack of facilities, expertise and money. Hence, duly planned hands-on- experience of at least 15 days, every semester, must be given to the students by inviting relevant experts and /or nominating a group of students to a desirable place where they can have hands-on-experience.

(d) We should have provision for training students at several selected training institutes.

(e) Students must be encouraged and funded to attend international conferences.

(f) Due economic incentives must be given to attract students to basic sciences both during the raining programme and in various jobs, later on.

References

1. Suresh Kumar, D, The New Indian Express, Education Supplement, 10th March 2006, p. 1.

2. Balaram, P., Curr. Sci. 2004, 86, 1583-1584

3. Balaram, P., Curr. Sci. 2001, 80, 601-602

Published: *Current Science*. Vol. 90. No. 9. 10 May 2006.

7

NKC Recommendations 2007 – Are they Really Going to Change the Scenario?

A.S. Rao

Before I quote form the NKC (National Knowledge Commission) report, let me mention a few lines from the archives of Current Science. In fact, these are the few lines that stirred the Editor (who is also attached to NKC) to initiate a debate which subsequently resulted in exposing the ills plaguing our academic and administrative institutes.

The scientific establishment is managed by a few extremely powerful people who:

(a) control most of the money

(b) are on all important job, promotion, and national committees, and

(c) decide what are the important scientific areas and directions to explore.

This coterie of science managers must travel ceaselessly to carry out its numerous commitments and therefore those who control science have neither the time to visit laboratories nor read scientific papers, not to speak, of course of doing experiments or themselves writing papers. Yet it is essential for them to give the appearance of being India's leading scientists. They must thus go about creating myths to give substance to their pretensions. To do so they engage in a very egregious form of gimmickry, including distributing scientific honours and laurels amongst themselves.

In subsequent debates, no one tried to refute the above opinions, although many expressed opinions that differed on other matters. Hence, it is quite legitimate to ask: Can NKC recommendations change the above scenario? It will not be a surprise if IRAHE (Independent Regulatory Authority on Higher Education proposed by NKC) itself is taken over by the above coterie. Presume that 15 per cent GER (gross enrolment ratio), as desired by NKC, is achieved by 2015. In other words, 85 per cent of the eligible population would still be deprived of enrolment. And one would still find the same rhetoric as of now in 2015 as well, from various groups of people and NKC constituted in 2015 would once again come up with the same three keywords expansion, equality and excellence. If the present numbers are inadequate, can doubling the number deliver the goods and achieve excellence? Without appreciating the basic problems and ground realities in the already existing institutions, what is the point in starting more number of institutions? Is it not tantamount to accepting the failure of the giant UGC system of university education and research? Even with the present numbers, if more than one-third of the colleges and universities are non-viable five and a large number of the remaining in different states of survival, how can further expansion achieve excellence? Just because there is a heavy increase of budget, some steps to sharing resources are suggested? This increase in budget and other steps no doubt were required even to strengthen the already existing number of institutions and provide quality education to the existing numbers. In fact, even in 1994 a requirement of at least 50,000 dollars per faculty member per year had been suggested. So the recommended expansion in education and the accompanying increase in budget would once again result in the same overall quality and situation as is present now. It is a well-known fact that out of the total budget, a lot (70–90 per cent) would go to brick and mortar, salaries and maintenance, etc. with little left to \impart training or to do any sensible research. To use the exact phrase of the author four, 'leaving precious little for the *raison d'etre*, namely teaching, research and development. Of course, it has one major advantage. It will keep the social unrest at a lower level. Keeping the unemployed and unemployable youth engaged in higher education is a good strategy to contain the youth and social unrest.

Let me end by appreciating some lines from the NKC Report. The remark by the NKC chairman in the foreword; 'Our country is too large, too complex and too diverse for "one size fits all" solutions'. It is implied in this statement that whatever you may suggest to the best of your integrity and calibre, there will always be enough number of people to oppose and sabotage what you suggest, because it genuinely does not fit them. Hence, it is probably better that we have separate policies framed, keeping in view the state of affairs in different zones of the country. May be a similar idea is reflected in the NKC Chairman's statement, 'At present we are engaged in discussions with about 17 states . . . . Hope at the end of these discussions another report would highlight the specific policies being adopted in different states.

Secondly, NKC has rightly pointed out to provide access to Government-held data. 'Data from different sectors need to be analysed holistically so that planning becomes more data-driven and reflects the ground situation. This means that data that are traditionally collected and managed separately, unrelated to each other, should now be seen together.' Hope the Editor and others would make use of RTI (right to information) as recommended by NKC and publish the above-required data in Current Science and once again initiate a debate, which I feel would be far more useful to the nation.

References

1. www.knowledgecommission.gov.in/reports/report07
2. Mahajan, S. M. , Curr. Sci., 1994, 67, 503–508.
3. Burma, D. P., Curr. Sci., 1994, 67, 681–682.
4. Balasubramanian, D., Curr. Sci., 1994, 67, 512–515.
5. Srivatsava, P. N., Curr. Sci., 1994, 67, 508–512.

Published: *Current Science*, Vol. 94, No. 10, 25 May 2008

8

Some Comments on RUSA (*Rashtriya Uchchatar Shiksha Abhiyan*)

A.S. Rao

RUSA (Rashtriya Uchchatar Shiksha Abhiyan) document is a heavy one dwelling on the future of higher education in our country. It is said that in planning commission many documents printed on expensive glossy paper are lying idle just because they have not taken into consideration ground realities and the feasibility of execution. Hope RUSA document does not become one such. A serious reading will lead to many comments which I have compiled here. The order in which my comments appear follows the order of matter presented in the document. The whole document is not covered but only the main statements.

1. The 12th plan wants to focus on Global needs—Since our country cannot absorb all, many would have to go to foreign countries and Hence, there is need to know the global needs and accordingly train our people to have ashare in the international job market. Further, we have to train our manpower to our country's needs. Take the Chinese, they are able to manufacture so many goods and flood our country and other countries. Why our country is not able to do that with such a large population and unemployment?
2. Whatever may be the increase in budget, since our country is vast the money distribution per institute would be thin if

the funds are to be allocated to all and nothing worthwhile may come out.

3. Recruitment of faculty in a department is presently an ill planned exercise and the department constitutes a random assortment of faculty. It should be a highly planned one. It should match with the curriculum of the various programs being offered by the department. Adequate number of faculty members must be there from different fields of specialisation matching the curriculum of the programs being offered. Running programs with poorly paid and temporary faculty with compromised qualifications is detrimental. It is not uncommon to start programs with fancy names and many of them are poorly viable and should be stopped.

   To enable the teachers to do their best they should not be heavily loaded with teaching responsibilities as they wish to do research and also have to attend to day to day administrative and academic activities. RUSA aims to start universities exclusively for research and Innovation. On the same lines it can start universities exclusively for teaching and training to roll out students who can be employable and also serve as motivated research scholars.The present universities depending on their state of affairs may be carved into exclusively teaching and research universities. The present system which emphasises both research and teaching in the same university only is leading to poor research and teaching, barring exceptions. UGC administrative structure and responsibility should be such that they can effectively monitor every university along with its affiliated colleges.

4. Every research goal has a specific time, capital and expertise dimension. Accordingly funding must be granted. Granting funds without taking into consideration the above parameters is just a waste of money. There should be a difference between the type of projects granted to traditional, agricultural, veterinary and medical institutes. Duplication

and overlapping of projects must be avoided and there should be a monitoring mechanism for that.

5. It is a welcome move that planning commission is focusing on public state universities. However, it should realise that their number is large and they area at different stages of growth and development. Hence, a proper survey has to be taken of public state universities and then only decide the magnitude and the head under which funding can be given.

6. That GER is only 18.8 per cent need not be highly depressing in view of our vast population. 18.8 per cent in terms of absolute numbers is significant. We surpass many advanced countries in terms of absolute numbers. To increase GER for rural areas and females distance education may be strengthened. As stated 94 per cent of the students are enrolled in state higher educational system. Central and national institutes are well funded with few students. Some of the national institutes take only Ph.D students who would carry out research work for their respective scientists. It is the student's work that goes in the name of the scientists work report. Hence, it is more apt to call them science supervisors or managers. By themselves they may not do any bench work. The same situation in state universities. The teachers are supervisors rather than bench workers and in case they neglect teaching for the sake of supervision, teaching suffers.

   When there are so many well-funded central and national institutes to pursue research goals, is it possible for the state universities to compete for the same research goals?

7. Vocational training must be strengthened and expanded.The candidates so rolled out can be employed in our country, abroad or can take up self-employment.

8. While increasing the GER is important, indiscriminately increasing the number of higher educational institutes with scant regard to the expenditure required to train the students should not be allowed. A blue print must be made to start

a higher educational institute. To make up for the shortage of funds state universities often distribute degrees through distance mode to raise the funds, there by bringing disrepute to the institute. It is better if distance education is disconnected form the universities and brought under a different umbrella of "Open and distance education universities".

9. The report has rightly emphasised the burden universities have to face because of affiliated institutions. The best way is to make unitary type universities. The colleges can be autonomous and made degree awarding institutes or Directorate of collegiate education be empowered to confer degrees.

10. Another major issue is how long higher education remains a concurrent subject? It is high time that it is made either exclusively a state subject or a central subject.

11. The present rule of not giving grants to institutions which are not 12B and 2F compliant is right. If this rule is not there, states indiscriminately start universities for the sake of regional or social appeasement. States also should invest reasonable amount of money in starting a university before expecting grants from UGC.

12. Transmitting money directly to the institute is the right method. Because greater the intermediaries greater will be the transmission losses and delay in distribution.

13. RUSA says that it will fund based on performance. But performance is based on the availability of funds! Hence, a reasonable amount of money must be initially provided.

14. UGC should see that in every state university the teacher to non-teaching staff to student ratios is more or less equal.

15. As per the report 316 state public universities i.e. nearly one universities for every two districts in the country! Not an inadequate number. We have done well. And if we take into consideration private universities as well we have one

university for one district in the country! So the problem is of skewed distribution. The universities are located in the metros and urban areas making the students to migrate and study and many are not able to do so. Hence, further growth should be concentrated in district headquarters and taluqs and /or provide financial assistance to candidates. Alternatively distance education mode had to be implemented extensively.

16. Another problem of skewed distribution is the number of colleges affiliated to a university. This is there only with some universities. The average number of state colleges affiliated to state universities is only 41 per university as per the document. In case private universities are allowed to affiliate colleges then with 634 universities and 33,023 colleges the average number of colleges per university would be only around 51.

17. RUSA aims to provide greater autonomy to universities. In what way the present autonomy prevents a VC to do or undo anything which he likes? Autonomy to university means autonomy to only one person i.e. VC. Hence, some amount of decentralisation must be there.

18. To improve the teaching learning process, the number of hours to be taught per paper must be increased at the same time the number of papers to be studied in a semester must be less. Presently there are many holidays in an academic year and each university has its own pattern of credit load per semester and calculating of working days. A fresh recommendation form UGC is required in this regard.

19. Across the country the number of faculty in a department varies a lot and UGC has no comments on this situation. In view of many programs being multidisciplinary, knowledge intensive and experimental oriented, a minimum of ten faculty members must be there in science departments. Further, the appointments may be made through state Public service commissions or state university recruitment boards. The university can simply recommend in which field of specialisation the post is required after examining the departmental profile and current needs.

20. Quality education requires emphasis on teaching and training of the students who would then turn out to be highly motivated for research and employment in different sectors.Teaching should be considered on par with research for career advancement. Otherwise research commitment would be an excuse to neglect UG/PG teaching thereby rolling out students with poor academic back ground.

21. RUSA aims to remove inequities to access to higher education among different social groups. When reservation is being strictly followed why there would be inequities? Since the broad social groups OC, OBC, SC, and ST in turn contain several castes, it may not be possible to cater to every caste in every social group. To bring in religious minorities, reservations based on religion have to be brought in. Lack of affordability is another factor which leads to inequities. Hence, fee waivers and scholarships have to be provided. If the aim of RUSA is to provide access to education to everyone who desires then it is a gargantuan task and the fund allotment must be increased many fold.

22. RUSA wants to modify Acts and statutes of universities. Is it not possible for all universities in a state to have common Acts and Statutes? Similarly a common curriculum for different subjects?

23. Though the governing bodies of universities like syndicate etc. are well balanced, there is considerable absenteeism of members when a meeting is called foreven when vital decisions are to be discussed. The decisions are taken with the minimum quorum. Autonomy cannot be delinked from accountability which is possible only if Government nominees are serious in the syndicate meetings. State higher education council chairman/secretary should be made a member of the syndicate if it is not already so.

In view of the large expansion in private institutions, there is a large representation form them in the senate. It is better if only one representative for the whole private institutions become a member rather one from each college.

24. Recruitment policy cannot by pass reservation policy which is further likely to be increased/complicated because of religious minority's reservations. It is better if the reservation policy is restricted to the entry level. Similarly communal considerations should not decide the appointment of a VC.

25. The decision taken on a file should be written with own hands of the concerned authority and then sign. Not simply sign on the note put up by the office staff. This makes the authority more responsible.

26. A well-equipped central instrumentation cell duly staffed must be there in every university. This should be funded by the UGC.

27. The desire to come up in the ladder makes one compromise with the ideals. Hence, time bound promotions may be introduced. Funding pattern is highly skewed. Most of the teachers have very little funds with which they do some tit-bits of research which does not contribute to the advancement of science. Can all the teachers inall the universities be funded for the whole life time? If not why should one expect a big research output form every faculty?

28. Government funding without some tags is undesirable. Expenditure must be duly ascertained.

29. Usually many files and data are created Just before the NAAC accreditation. Hence, it must be made mandatory to have an annual check-up internally. All components of all activities must be duly computerised.

30. It is clear form Annexure II that salaries account for most of the expenditure and very little is then available for doing experiments in the curriculum, research project works of M.Sc. and M.Phil students etc. Hence, the compromise in training. Either the project work should be banned or sufficient money be allocated for the purpose. The number of the students admitted may accordingly be decided.

31. The best way to avoid malpractices—this may sound eccentric but there is no other way—in the appointment of VC's is to select a person from the concerned university itself on the basis of seniority for a limited tenure. Then there will be malpractices to manipulate the seniority parameter alone. Hence, university should maintain a seniority list at the university level and UGC recommendations be strictly followed to include past services so that seniority is rightly fixed. In case a VC has to come from outside he should from a state public university system from the main campus and not from any other system.

32. Universities should be cosmopolitan and should have significant number of students who are ethnically from different states and international students. In particular international students to be given special attention during their stay.

33. To become a world class university both teaching and research must be equally emphasised.

34. At a glance it appears that there is no strict direct correlation between GER and per capita income in the state universities. Secondly it appears that in smaller states the correlation is better and GER is high. Hence, it appears that smaller states are better for the future of education and to realise the vision of RUSA document.

Published: University Today, 2014, 34(6), 7-8.

9

Some Comments on the Inclusive and Qualitative Expansion in Higher Education during 12th Five Year Plan

A.S. Rao

'This document has significant number of points mentioned in another UGC's document "Proceedings of the vice chancellors of central and state universities". The document discusses an ambitious plan of action for achieving three objectives in the 12th FYP; Viz; access and expansion, equity and inclusion and quality and excellence. Though the working group has discussed both pros and cons still the following points need to be pondered.

A. Many target groups have been left out

Five more target groups need to be considered, viz; Transgender, street children and children of red light areas, orphans and economically backward classes irrespective of the social group. Though SC's are covered, since long there is a demand by Dalit Christians to be given a reservation. After the analysis of the recent census, the scenario may further change.

Further, there are so many categories of people who for the sake of livelyhood are already in different jobs, which are low paid and long hours of working. These people also want to grow educationally Hence, a plan of action be worked out for these people, with consultations from ESI (employees state insurance) and labour department.

B. Degrees are irrelevant without a job

A more important point under inclusiveness is to recognise that caste is a harsh fact of Indian life and the vast social heterogeneity within a broad social group. For example, there are more than 3000 castes under OBC's. Some states have further split OBC's. Even then there a huge number of castes left out in getting the benefits of reservation. Presently we do not know who among the above castes are able to take advantage of under OBC reservation. Even under SC's there are many groups. Further, there are many groups currently agitating for getting them included under OBC, SC/ST etc. Therefore, GER of various castes must be known and preference should be given to those castes whose GER is presently low. Further, what is the use of degrees if they cannot fetch a lively hood? Recently in Rajasthan, in one of the universities, PG's and Ph.D.'s have applied for a peon's post. Hence, increasing GER should be matched with the type and number of jobs available in our country and abroad and this information should be made public.

C. Over expectation is self-deception and misleading

While the objectives are noble and some may materialise, it is too ambitious to expect a quantum jump in quality and excellence. Even with the present number quality and excellence is not up to the desired level how can it be there with doubling the GER. We may have a horizontal expansion but not a vertical rise in standards.

D. Caste system among universities

UGC has introduced a new caste system among the universities; Navarathna universities, Innovative universities, universities with potential for excellence and the remaining (Shudra universities) This fourfold classification demoralises the huge number of universities. If a university is functioning well, give them grants, but why to categorise under a different name? Moreover self-proclaimed titles will not be regarded so much. Let others comment on our universities. Moreover, for decades no university of ours figures in the top in the global ranking. Then what is the point in ourselves giving titles that too prematurely? Long-time back an idea was mooted. Bringing all the national stalwarts under one roof. If such a thing can be done (unlikely because, two stalwarts cannot see eye to eye in our country) one can understand the title of Navarathna universities. The proposal for innovative universities, that too 14, is really surprising. It is indirectly saying that all the universities are doing routine, confirmatory research and are not innovative. If all the present universities have failed, the possibility that the new comers would bring laurels is remote. Suppose a university is given the title of 'potential for excellence ", it is like a philosophical statement that "every soul is potentially divine". But the ultimate aim is to manifest this divinity. If excellence is not achieved in a certain period of time the above title must be withdrawn.

E. Inadequate money to develop infrastructure gives an exaggerated low student to land ratio

The low student to land area ratio is actually the result of old norms of UGC which wanted a huge acreage to start a new university. Now UGC itself has relaxed this norms. In the surplus land, in addition to expanding the existing university we can also start another university or a college or may be utilised for agriculture whose products may go the students mess. Except for old universities now it is not possible to get vast tracts of land in urban areas. So vertical growth is inevitable or the university has to be located in far suburban areas or emerging town ships. Paradoxically in many universities many faculty and departments are struggling/fighting for space, for research and teaching labs, class rooms. Further, all universities do not have equally well developed play grounds, faculty guest houses, hostels, hospitals etc. Hence, student to land ratio must be reworked.

F. Do not always compare in terms of percentages. Look at the absolute numbers too

We should not compare our GER or other parameters with

other countries always as a percentage in view of highly contrasting population of countries. We have only 2.4% of geographical land but 18% of world's population. So even 1% of our population is equal 100% of some other countries and 25% of our population is equivalent to hundred % of USA's population. Therefore, we should also try to compare in terms of absolute numbers. In terms of absolute numbers we are a large number as compared to many countries. Are the present numbers of scientists had been /or inadequate to bring laurels to the country? Look at the world renowned multinationals in house R and D's. The number of scientists vary from few hundred to few thousand. The rest is supporting staff. They bring laurels to their country. A similar set up and environment may be built up in our country.

G. What should be our priority?

To increase GER or to increase food supply to the huge and growing population? How to feed well, 121 crore people who are further expected to grow till around 2050, particularly when the land holdings are less, per capita land availability is decreasing, diversion of agricultural land for non-agricultural purposes is increasing and people are migrating from agriculture to other professions? Food distribution also is faulty. In this scenario—God forbid—a civil war in future is not unlikely. It is high time that India, by law, ear mark due proportion of land towards agriculture and prevent diversion of agricultural land to other purposes... Absentee land lordism, keeping the land fallow, should not be permitted. Making school education free along with two meals followed by vocational training is a more promising strategy to prepare people for employment. In the inclusive growth, farmers and other low paid jobs related to agriculture have to be given specific attention.

H. Quality faculty are different from committed faculty

Though the faculty has all the calibre, they may not be committed to teaching as it no way helps them in further growth in terms of power and pelf. Hence, they are busy with research, administration and related activities and outsourcing if possible.

That teaching is a primary duty even in university too, is never emphasised by apex bodies and even if it is emphasised, teachers are not in a position to follow it due to above mentioned reasons. Neglect of teaching is being encouraged by statements of the working group like "A university contribution to knowledge is in the form of publications it has made in the field of research and the number of research degrees that are awarded." etc. If that is, so what is the difference between a research institute and a university? Why should we start UG and PG programmes in a university in large numbers if teaching is not emphasised? It is embarrassing to listen to the comment that education by distance mode is better than a regular one! Because in the distance mode definitely certain fixed number of classes are conducted without fail and notes also are given. Neither of that is mandatory in a regular course. Faculty strength in many colleges particularly in private colleges is less because of UGC's stipulation of unrealistic teaching load. With just two faculty also they can run one two year programme and they are still within the frame work of rules and regulations. Sometime in universities too such a situation may prevail. At the most they may have three. There is no difference of teaching work load between colleges and universities though the latter have a big research mandate which is not expected from the college teacher. However, in their own interest and partly due to UGC's pressure, college teachers too involve in research. Arts and humanities people do not get as much funds as science departments. Hence, any marks for "grants received" must have a different yard stick for arts and humanities.

I. Conduct refresher and orientation programmes during the vacation period

Academic staff colleges should run their refresher and orientation programmes during the vacation period and not during the working semesters. Teachers attending these courses are away from their teaching responsibilities and alternative arrangements are seldom made. Similarly a large number of seminars and conferences etc., are conducted at the expense of classes.

J. No freedom of speech to evaluate

In the evaluation of teachers by the students, I do not know why Ph.D students are excluded from evaluating their guides? Anyhow, in either case is it possible for the students to give negative remarks about their teachers and guides? In the west it may be possible but not in India. Leave aside students, even parents are afraid to tell anything adverse about the system, lest their wards will be penalised for that.

K. CBCS system must be made uniform

CBCS system demands that the question paper pattern must be such that students should have full opportunities to score maximum grades. Further, by the time students attempt their final exams they should not feel any stress. In our country the marks for internal evaluation and external evaluation vary a lot, and we have -4 to 10 point system with different number of grades. There should be at least one holiday between two exams. All the recommended books for a programme -one set, preferably two-should be kept in the reference section of the general library.

L. In built checks needed

Good governance is a matter of commitment—a matter of mind and heart - and is not dependent on computers. Hence, some in built checks must be there, in addition to selecting a right man for the post.

M. Universities should not be burdened with constituent colleges

Constituent colleges may be located on the campus if space is available but they should be under the "Directorate of collegiate education" and it may be empowered to confer degrees. Alternatively UGC may take a bold step of making all colleges autonomous with the right to confer degrees. Let them perform and survive. Why should they sell themselves with the university name?

N. Table 2 may be upgraded

Table 2 indicating the state-wise number of universities should have included the total population of the states and population in the age group of 18-23. If the above data is not available it should be generated. After the completion of the census it may be done.

Published: University Today, 2012, 32(5), 5.

10

Suggestions for the Improvement of Parliamentary Bills on Education

A.S. Rao

Four bills pertaining to education were introduced in the parliament whose details have been published in University news (2011, Vol. 49, pp. 2-58.). All these bills are signed by the Hon'ble Minister for MHRD Kapil Sibal* and are in need of suggestions for improvement. The following suggestions need to be pondered for implementation.

A. The National Accreditation Regulatory Authority for Higher Educational Institutions Bill, 2010.

Chapter 1

1.2. As to why this bill is not applicable to J&K alone is not mentioned and Hence, no feedback can be given on this point. This condition is also there for some other bills. 2.0, as to why this bill is not applicable to all but for agricultural education and research, is not clear. In principle ICAR MCI (Medical Council of India), Dental council of India, Veterinary council of India, CSIR, UGC and AICTE can take care of their respective institutes in matters of accreditation and these bodies can be monitored by the "The National Accreditation Regulatory Authority for Higher Educational Institutions (TNARAHEI)" and guided for the

*Presently Hon'ble Smriti Irani

accreditation process. How about accreditation of space, atomic energy and defence institutes?

Chapter III

5.3. Though the Head office be at Delhi, there should be branch offices in all the four zones of the country (north, south, east and west).7.1-3- Qualifications for appointment of chair person may need to be reviewed. Why the compulsion of 25 yrs of service and 55 years of age and should be a Vice chancellor or Head of institute? When the retirement age is not uniform in the country varying from 58-65, when the entry of a person into service is getting late (the age limit for a lecturer post is 45 yrs. and there are people joining as a lecturer around that age), when UGC says that an outstanding candidate may be appointed as a professor irrespective of his little service, why all the above stipulations? Professors who could or did not become a VC or a Head of the institution are they inferior to the above? Hence, eligibility requirements for the chair person post may be revised to include qualified people irrespective of whether one is a VC or Head of the institution and reduce the service experience requirement form 25 to 15 years similar situation is there in some other bills.

7.3. The four members to be chosen must represent the four zones of the country and the states may be rotated within the zones after every term. Women to be appointed (6.0) can be in addition to the four mentioned in 7.3 taking the total to 5.

8. Very often the cabinet secretary's office tenure is short and they may not be there for a long time in the post. So frequently there has to be changes. Hence, a cabinet secretary may be the chair person only if he has at least 3Yrs in his office. Otherwise a senior most IAS who has at least three years of service left may be appointed as a chair person and cabinet secretary may be an additional member. Similar problem can be there for secretary to MHRD if he is transferred. Composition of the authority should not change frequently before the term expires. Therefore, experts with the required amount of service only should be selected.

8d. When agricultural institutions are exempted in this act (Chapter I, 2) what is the need of selecting an expert in the field of agriculture education and research? Agricultural institutes presently affiliated to traditional universities should be disconnected and be brought under the nearest agricultural university. In any case there is a post of DDG, ICAR in education who can be the member.

9.1. Our country being vast, heterogeneous and with a large academic community, the tenure of office of 5Yrs may be reduced to 3Yrs, so that many people get an opportunity to function. Similar situation is there in some other bills.

9.2. All the members should have the benefit of tax free salary and allowances along with non-taxable perks like free housing, conveyance, medical allowance, children's education allowance etc. All the members, irrespective of the previous salary drawn should draw equal salary as members. Further, as they are not allowed to engage in any employment, they may be duly compensated by way of salary.

16. It is not clear as to how many accreditation agencies the authority wants to approve. This job may be left to individual agencies like NAAC, ICAR, MCI, VCI etc. keeping in view the number of institutes to be accredited and the frequency with which they are to be accredited. Bar councils can be brought into picture for accrediting the law colleges and universities. The TNARAHEI can peruse the applications of the accreditation agencies forwarded by the above mentioned individual agencies and approve the same and can finally formulate the evaluation proforma after receiving the inputs from individual agencies and monitor and guide them from time to time. (Statement of Object and reasons 2).

11. A person who is on deputation can always return to his parent institution after the tenure expires and it is quite possible that during his tenure he might have to deliberate a case from his parent institute. Hence, this rule may be modified. At the most he may not be allowed to deliberate in such cases as mentioned in

12, and another member may be temporarily substituted for that case. Similar situation is there in some other bills.

21. Alternatively TNARAHEI can select eminent academicians and support them to establish an accreditation agency.

B. The Educational Tribunals Bill, 2010.

Chapter I

General Points

I. Emphasis should be on the motto "Prevention is better than cure" rather than a dispute coming to the tribunal. For this MHRD should ensure:

   a. Uniformity of rules and regulations and acts and statutes among the institutes. Otherwise comparisons and contrasts ultimately may lead to case filing.

   b. That rules should be stated simply and unambiguously without any loop holes. If they are also simultaneously made in respective vernacular, there would be absolutely no scope for subjectivity either in English or in vernacular.

   c. Arbitrary and discretionary powers and special case phenomenon should be minimised.

   d. All financial matters should be settled in the same financial year and nothing should be pending.

   e. A notification to all institutes for continuous updating of their web sites with all details as specified by the regulatory authorities and in a manner useful to students, parents and general public.

   f. Students prospectus should not have anything hidden and must be complete in all respects. It should be able to serve as a basis for filing a case by parents/students, if need be.

g. In case the tribunal rejects the case but the person wins the case in Supreme Court, the tribunal should bear the entire cost incurred by the person.

II. Emphasis should be on the motto "justice delayed is justice denied". Imagine thc man has to first exhaust all the remedies, then come to thc state tribunal, followed by national tribunal and then the Supreme Court! How much time it is going to take? Hence, a reasonable time limit be fixed and after its lapse the case should be decided in favour of the person.

Chapter II: State Educational Tribunal

As in the TNARAHEI four members must be there. Only two are inadequate. A Government may change during the tenure of the committee. In such cases does the new Government has the right to change the committee or the same committee can continue?

Chapter III

C. National Educational Tribunal

21.2. Since eight members are to be selected, two from each of the four national zones may be selected.

21.3. Two to three women to be appointed should represent different zones.

35. The provision of appealing to President of India should be there, in case a person loses his case in Supreme Court.

General Points

The tribunal should not take a wrong precedent as a valid criteria for taking a favourable decision. Rather, the tribunals should place on record that it was a wrong precedent, so that in future such decisions will not be taken

The prohibition of Unfair Practices in Technical Educational Institutions, Medical Educational Institutions and universities Bill, 2010.

Chapter II

3. Private institutes should work out the financial requirements for running a programme/the institute as per the desired standards and the same be approved by state and national tribunals. Similarly the margin of profit be approved. Action may be taken only if the above approved limit is crossed.
5. In the prospectus hostel fees also should be mentioned. A commonly prevalent grievance at PG and M.Phil level, both in public and private institutes is the students pay fees for all the semesters but they are not funded by the respective institute to carry out their mandatory research project in their final semester. They are driven to seek projects elsewhere by paying money both officially and /or unofficially towards the cost of their projects. Of course, there are some institutes which do not charge anything but oblige the students? Since the number of students is very large, those who fall under the former category are a large majority.
7. The procedure of depositing the original certificates with the institutes either by the students or the faculty should be stopped. If a candidate with draws before the date of commencement of course as mentioned in the prospectus, or does not attend any class, full fees should be refunded.

Chapter III

10. Besides penalty, the authority should be able to refund the capitation fees to the students.

Blanket exemption for minority institutions is not desirable. Two broad groups are religious and linguistic. Both are there in every state. In case they all start colleges that would be huge number not coming under the purview of the Bills. Lastly but not the least, the Government should take cognizance of the fact that private institutes are run by a wide range of big shots VIZ; God men, Businessmen, politicians, bureaucrats, cine actors etc. Is it possible to take stringent steps as mentioned in the bill? Further, when we want GER (gross enrolment ratio), to what extent Government wants private sector to contribute towards this goal?

In case the Government alone can do it, it is fine. If not, the private players, Indian or foreign have to be listened too.

D. The Foreign Educational Institutions (Regulation of entry and operations) Bill, 2010.

Chapter II

General

(a) Our government should sponsor some of our students to the above institutes after conducting an entrance test etc.

(b) Salaries should be paid in foreign currency and be tax free 5. At least 10 per cent of the students and 25 per cent of the faculty should be from the country which is providing the education to ensure greater credibility for the institution.

Published: University Today, 2012, 32(14), 5.

B. About Indian Science

11

What is Wrong with Indian Science? A Bouquet of Opinions by Eminents Scientists from all over the Country. To What Extent we are Different Today?

A.S. Rao

An NRI physicist by name S.M. Mahajan from USA happened to write to the then PM V.P. Singh during early nineties that India does not possess a single university of international repute and proposed to form a "National Science university". (That we still don't rank in the top in the global rankings is a harsh fact). In 1994 his views and proposal was published in current science, Bangalore* and a long debate ensued thereafter on this view point. The proposal was finally turned down. However, during this process a large number of eminent scientists from across the country have expressed their opinions during 1994-1995. In this article nothing is mine, from beginning to end. All statements have been excerpted from the articles published incurrent science during the above debate by eminent scientists across the country (Except for the captions). Before I mention the points excerpted let me in short, tell Dr S.M. Mahajan's views on Indian science, which forced him to make the proposal

*Bengaluru

and initiate a debate." ....The scientific establishment is managed by a few extremely powerful people who: (a) control most of the money (b) are on all important job, promotion and national committees, and (c) decide what are the important scientific areas and direction to explore. This coterie of science managers must travel ceaselessly to carry out its numerous commitments and therefore, those who control science have neither the time to visit laboratories nor read scientific literature, not to speak of course of doing experiments or themselves writing the papers. Yet, it is essential for them to give the appearance of being India's leading scientists. They must thus go about creating myths to give substance to their pretensions. To do so they engage in a very egregious form of gimmickry including : (a) distributing scientific honours and laurels amongst themselves, and (b) giving totally lopsided assessment of our current scientific state with needless to say all the exaggeration and untruths, giving a rather favourable impression of the state....."

Now once again for the 12th Five Year Plan and evolving a new science policy so many committees have been formed and many approach papers/bills/ documents have been made. The point is, to what extent we are now different compared to mid-nineties? The below mentioned points must be taken into consideration while framing polices for the 12th FYP and for evolving a new science policy.

Here, an effort has been made here to list out the various opinions expressed by scientists from all over the country during 1994-1995. The order in which they have been listed does not in any way indicate the importance of the opinions. All these have to be definitely pondered over by people from all walks of life, and compare and contrast with the present state of affairs to evolve a new science policy.

A. Educational institutes are not sacrosanct

1. To pretend that there are no malpractices and malafide in the practice and management of science in India is to ignore the obvious.

2. Large scale tampering with selection process of both teachers and students has contributed to mediocrity in our educational system, which can only multiply mediocrity and cannot create excellence.
3. Compromises make more compromises necessary and all these compromises spoil the system.
4. Other than appointing committees after committees we have not taken any concrete action to over haul the system.
5. Science establishment is perceived to be run by a few extremely powerful people whose commitment and calibre is highly questionable.
6. Irrespective of the students merit or funds or facilities available, teachers continue to roll out Ph.D's only for the sake of their bio-data.
7. Our teacher-cum-scientists in the universities are usually carried away by the fads of the day. For example, in each and every place we try to start courses on molecular biology, biotechnology etc. with extreme disregard to adequate facilities. So what all that has happened is new name plates and boards have come up all over.
8. Students do not get marks for what they write but what an examiner decided they should get, whether the latter knows the subject or not.

B. Biased, incomplete and limitations of funding

6. There is no continuity in the funding. Hardly any project can be completed to fruition.
7. With large chunks of money going to wrong people and projects and the fierce fighting for the remaining peanuts has resulted only in producing Ph.D's and papers and nothing else. A large number of teachers in the universities remain almost without any funds for a greater part of their life.
8. Private industries contribution to research funding is negligible. This is not so in west.

9. Mere increase in the allocation of funds cannot provide technological excellence.
10. More than 70 per cent (often as much as 90 per cent) of the budget of a university is spent on salaries and maintenance, leaving precious little for the raison *d'etre*, namely teaching, research and development.

C. No standard and innovative teaching and evaluation

11. The Indian university even at its best is not structured to train the pupils to think, question and investigate critically.
12. We do not know how to distinguish and evaluate scientists, teachers, science managers, technicians, research scholars and students.
13. There is absence of any distinction between scientists and technicians. Can anyone become a scientist? Nurses and pharmacists do not become doctors on the basis of seniority. Why is there no such distinction in science?
14. Colleges and Universities are generally extensions of schools in mentality and structure.
15. Primary and secondary level education system in our country needs thorough modification in every aspect.
16. The sorry state of under graduate and the quality of graduate education in our universities is well documented.
17. The research taken up is more inspired by what is happening in the developed world and which was driven by their needs and not ours.
18. Our universities and institutes at the most serve as manpower export centres.
19. Experimental science is in doldrums because the laboratories have no equipment or antiquated equipment.
20. Our universities have multiplied and have become mostly inefficient degree awarding machines with scant regard for vital societal obligations.

21. It is true that our educational system is almost collapsing.
22. There is practically no monitoring of the quality of research or teaching.
23. We admit several fold more number of students than what we should in our educational institutions.
24. Probably by the time a student join the Post Graduate or even under graduate, considerable damage has already occurred to the student and his prospects of development are bleak.

D. Do our scientists carry out any bench work?

25. Indian science has only generals. No soldiers. Whatever may be the calibre, students and post docs are our soldiers and not the scientists.

E. Is this pessimism (or right inference?) still there?

26. It has never been possible to do good science in India and no change appears to be in sight.

F. Do we do any original and innovative research?

27. 95 per cent (Ninety five per cent) of India's research is a follow up research and any person making tall claims must be viewed with caution. In fact, most our research is of confirmatory nature.

G. Miserable plight of universities and colleges

28. Today, about one-third of the universities and colleges are non-viable.

H. A God father is a must to rise in academics

29. Whom you know is more important than what you know.

I. How long this situation will prevail?

30. We do not have even one university which can be compared to the west in the world over all.

J. How long this dependency?

31. Manufacturing of sophisticated research equipment has never

been considered seriously in this country, and we have miserably failed in the area of fine chemicals for modern research.

K. Absence of unity and coherence and convergence

32. The present scenario is depressing not only because of government indifference to science but as a consequence of the scientific community's ability to work collectively and purposefully towards common goals.

L. A role for MHRD

33. We have to have a serious review of the charter and function of the UGC.

M. Are science departments so innocent?

34. The troubles of the universities mostly originate (not always) from the arts a, law and social sciences departments.

N. Our country is too much diverse

35. It is not reasonable or meaningful to provide one line summary solutions to the ails of S & T (Science and Technology) having an aetiology related to the history, socio-economics and politics of the land.

O. A fallacy

36. It is often stated that India has the third largest scientific man power of the world. This really is not true; for just having degrees in science does not make one a scientist.

P. Can we at least take pride in space, atomic energy and agriculture?

37. Whatever we have achieved in atomic energy, space and agriculture is adaptation and successful implementation of techniques already established elsewhere.

Q. Brain drain

38. Good students migrate to other countries or to other careers

within the country. Universities suffer another brain drain where students prefer to join national institutes for their Ph.D's.

R. Need for committed teachers

39. Teachers rarely care to update themselves qualitatively in all respects, resulting in the destruction of the graduate and post graduate education system.
40. The harm done to generations of students by a bad teacher is incalculable.

S. A social awareness of science is a must

41. The reasons for unsatisfactory scenario are as much sociological as scientific.
42. Unless an integrated effort is made to bring about a social change and to re-establish our social values, we cannot hope to improve and maintain a high level of science research.
43. Our society is unwilling to take clear cut decisions as to what it wants to do with its youth.
44. Many students opt for Ph.D programmes because of unemployment and not because of their interest or merit in science and after completing the degrees again science is just another source of employment. Education and science being the two most vital inputs for the development of society and country, is it not our responsibility to analyse all the above problems and swing into action honestly, collectively and with all our might in evolving a new education and science policy?

Acknowledgements

I wish to place on record my sincere appreciation for the calibre and commitment of the Editor and editorial office of Current Science, Bengalore* for running the above debate for a long time.

Published by: University Today, 2013, 33(1), 20.

---

*Bengaluru

12

Need for Useful Institutes rather than World Class Institutes, What else the Three Science Academies could have Deliberated?

A.S. Rao

Need for useful institutes rather than world class institutes

Periodically there is a debate on the standard of our educational institutes and ills plaguing our system. However, one thing needs to be acknowledged is, though we do not have world class institutes, there has been a tremendous expansion in education with 540 plus universities and 26000 colleges. They may vary a lot in quality but we can say that quantitatively we have made a big progress to cater to the needs of vast population. But even the present capacity is supposed to cater to only 12 per cent of the eligible candidates and there is a further need for a huge number of universities and colleges. According to Kapil Sibal* we require 1500 universities and 40-45 thousand colleges. Even then we fall short as compared to enrolment in western countries. Presently a huge number of good students are not able to enter Government institutes in view of their limited number and are forced to join private institutes shelling out lot of money. If they cannot afford either they have to change their career or land up

*Presently Hon'ble Smriti Irani.

in low grade institutes. Hence, government has a serious responsibility to invest a lot and cater to the needs of millions of aspirants for higher education. In such a scenario even in the near future we can only expect a quantitative improvement and not world class institutes or excellence.

Mark Taylor in a recent article in Nature (U.K) magazine has mentioned while commenting on the reforms in Ph.D system that "we must design curricula that focus on solving practical problems, such as providing clean water to a growing population". Therefore, Ph.Ds and academicians should work on existing problems of our country and academicians should preserve till they solve the problems. Once a scientist by name Bidwell said that 'useful discoveries are different from exciting discoveries" Our emphasis should be on making useful discoveries. Hence, our academicians should strive to identify and concentrate on the problems facing the country and provide solutions. A large number of problems faced by the country are mentioned in many sociology books in addition to scientific articles. Further, some problems identified by the world watch institute Washington are also relevant to us. With time we may keep identifying some more. Adequate and authentic classified information about the above problems and their current status must be clearly brought out and should become a part of our curricula of all streams of students. To tell in Mark Taylor's words our curricula should focus on our national problems and our teaching and research should be relevant to this curriculum. In this endeavour academicians from science and technology should work in coordination with academicians from arts and humanities. If we may follow the above approach even if we do not have world class institutes we will have institutes highly useful to the country solving the problems of the country and making it more stable and powerful.

Published: *Current Science*

13

What else the Three Science Academies could have Deliberated?

A.S. Rao

The position paper' is a worthwhile document and will serve as a basic document for future deliberations. I discuss here the position paper keeping life science programmes in mind. At the outset, I may say that any programme offered by the elite institutes like IISc, IISER, etc. or universities would be much sought after by the students. Students will give importance to the institutes and not bother about the duration of the course or the specialisation. Bright students pursuing the 4-year programme would be very happy as it would give them an opportunity to go abroad at the same time as their counterparts in BE/B Tech. Presently they are delayed by a year because of the 3 + 2 pattern.

After the science academies' initiative on Post-school Science Education, private institutions may find conducting the 4-year degree programme lucrative. Till now students have preferred the 3-year programme in disciplines such as Bio-technology/Bio-chemistry/Microbiology; it is quite possible that they may continue to prefer the same disciplines in a 4-year programme as well.

The position paper does not mention M.Phil anywhere. What is the stand of the joint science education panel with reference to M Phil degree? While recommending a lateral exit with an M.Sc. or M.Phil from an integrated Ph.D programme, the authors have made a statement, The difference between the two would be whether one has done a project (M.Phil) or not (M.Sc)'. It means that an M.Sc. degree may be earned purely by course work without any project work. In view of the large number of student'sinvolved, project work may be eliminated from the M.Sc. curriculum and replaced by some useful courses. But the problem is that presently M.Sc. with project work is the predominant pattern, and research institutes and foreign institutes prefer these students for Ph.D. It is not clear at what level the position paper recommend specialisation. On page 1417 it is stated that BSc degrees with specialisation must be stopped and on page 1418 it is stated that 'B.S. students will opt for a major subject in the last two years'. If there is no specialisation then the degree can be conferred in a broad manner, i.e., BS (Life Sciences or Biology). If there is specialisation then there are two ways of giving the degree. Say, for e.g., BS Life Sciences (Biochemistry) or BS (Biochemistry). In what way is the degree going to be conferred? There is a similar problem in offering the degree in integrated M Sc. The UGC's stipulation of a postgraduate (PG) degree in the relevant discipline for a lecturer's post means that specialisation at PG level is required for a lecturer's post. Can M.Sc. Life sciences (Microbiology) be equated with M.Sc. (Microbiology)?

Take the analogy of BDS (Bachelor of Dental Surgery). Here, students specialise soon after plus two and they read many subjects during the course. It is not unjustified to offer an undergraduate (UG) programme in century-old subjects like biochemistry or microbiology, etc.

In all different patterns; 3 + 2, 4 + 1, integrated 5-year M.Sc., integrated Ph.D after BSc/BS, the total duration for finishing M.Sc. is the same, i.e., five years. While all programmes, B.Sc, BS, M.Sc. and M.Phil are time-bound programmes, the only programme which is not time bound but extremely variable is Ph.D. Students are worried about this as they have to spend anywhere from three to six years to complete their Ph.D. The academies have not expressed any concern with respect to the duration of Ph.D. Many of our students go to Germany, Italy, etc. and finish their Ph.D's in three years and subsequently carry out their postdoc in the developed West. Why cannot our reputed institutes give a Ph.D in 3 years?

The desire 'to have a uniform pattern of post school education in the country' can be achieved only if education becomes entirely a state or central government subject and not concurrent. Keeping in view the numbers involved, how can the burden of UG, PG and Ph.D's be shared among colleges, universities and research institutes? Over load of multiple responsibilities will decrease the efficiency of both the individual and the organisation.

The position paper rightly states that 'there is a strong need for substantial improvement in the quality and quantity of teachers at college as well as university level'. For this to happen, the present mandatory credit hour load of teachers has to be reduced and accordingly additional recruitment has to be made. Further, we may take a leaf out of the system prevailing in agricultural universities. They have segregated the faculty into three streams, viz. teaching, research and extension. Though the administration can transfer anyone from one stream into another, any indiscriminate transfer is found to be highly unproductive, because the three streams require specific talents, aptitudes and commitment. In the traditional universities also this system could be followed. A certain number of faculty could be earmarked exclusively for teaching. If their lecturers fall short of the requirement, they may be supplemented with a few additional lecturers from the faculty involved in active research. To take care of the lab practical's, separate faculty like the position of a Demonstrator (below the lecturer level) as in olden days could be restored. In addition, or alternatively, adequate number of technicians could be employed. What type of administrative system can give the best deal to students, research scholars and faculty? The present administrative system is regarded as highly unfriendly.

The position paper has commented on colleges and universities but not on the state of affairs in the research institutes. How good and productive are they? Look at the MRC Lab in Cambridge. A single institute has won 29 Nobels till now! An annually recurring question is why our research institutes do not win Nobels? What is lacking? Funds? Expertise?

Venkatraman Ramakrishnan recently said that 'there is a lack of funds and world class laboratories to carry out research'. Paradoxically many of our research institutes in their advertisements mention that they have state of the art facilities, world class infrastructure, qualified and experienced faculty, etc. If so, then what is lacking?

Mashelkar commenting on Indian science blames the prevailing hierarchical systems, and the lack of freedom for students and others in having a questioning attitude. He says that 'out-of-the-box' thinking and healthy irreverence should be promoted. The three academies should deliberate and present a position paper on why our institutes do not get Nobels.

Published: *Current Science*, Vol. 98, No. 5, 10 March 2010

14

Indian Science Congress— Time for Reflection

P. Tauro and *A.S. Rao*

In the olden days, various scientific disciplines did not have their own associations and Hence, met under the banner of the Science Congress to discuss and out-line their vision for Indian science. Today, every discipline has its own association— some more than one — which holds annual or biannual, national and regional conferences, where the concerned scientists meet and discuss their work and draw out future plans for their discipline. Hence, the role of the Science Congress under these circumstances has become redundant.

It is now time that the Indian Science Congress Association changes the way the Congress is conducted. It was our first Prime Minister, Jawaharlal Nehru, who decided to attend the Congress every year and state his scientific vision for India. It was an exercise worth the effort, but some of the Prime Ministers who came after him have lacked his scientific temper. As a result, it has become an unwanted, routine affair for the Prime Minister. It is better that the Science Congress Association now makes this as an association meeting and reduce the cost and duration. They may invite the PM — if capable of stating his views on Indian science — to present his vision of Indian science, followed by a few lectures on selected themes by reputed scientists. This should be combined with the annual association activities, presentation of awards, felicitations, etc. All this can be done within two days at a reduced cost. The money saved can be used to encourage the Student Science Congress, which perhaps achieves more than what this bigger Science Congress does.

Published: *Current Science*, Vol. 94, No. 9, 10 May 2008

C. About University Vice Chancellors

15

Appointment of VCs and Politicisation of Academics

A.S. Rao

This is with reference to the views expressed by Virk and Basa, regarding the appointment of Vice Chancellors (VCs) and politicisation of academics. We should be happy that the underworld and other criminals have not yet started interfering in these appointments and other educational matters. But, it is not an unlikely situation in the near future in view of the hundreds of opinions expressed by all sections of the society, after the N. N. Vohra Committee report. Hence, the readers of Current Science have a greater responsibility in future.

Some say that 'from chaos emerges a new order. Presently it is chaos, which would increase in spite of all our writings in Current Science. Do readers remember the long debate during 1994-1995 on a National Science University? The readers should place on record their sincere appreciation for the calibre and commitment of the editor in this regard. In the above debate, academicians from all over the country have exposed so many things about the state of affairs of education and science and technology in our country. Rather, the situation has deteriorated a bit more, as is evident from the letters in these columns till today.

Virk and Basa say that politicians interfere in the appointment of VCs. Do they interfere only in the appointments of VCs? How about in the appointment of faculty and administrative staff? How about in the distribution of research grants and other funds, selection of national and international fellowships, student admissions, securing ranks, etc.? We keep hearing that politicians interfere even in the above. Of course, we also keep hearing that whatever that is left after the interference of politicians, is manipulated by so many others, which includes our fellow academicians.

Several years ago, in one particular region, the appointment of a VC in a university was stalled, because there arose a question 'why is a person from only one particular social group appointed as a VC every time? The 'Social Assertiveness has increased manifold and is going to further increase, the consequences of which will be reflected in so many ways. Already we are witnessing it in the form of various appointments, fragmentation of districts and states, emergence of political parties with affiliation to social groups, coalition governments, etc. So, whenever a VC post is vacant, it is only natural that politicians are to intervene. Hence, the appointment of a VC is not purely political, but it is based on socio-political considerations'. In the above process, often the faculty of the respective institutions take an active part. Sometimes there may be an added dimension of `economic considerations. This is an outcome of increased commercialisation of education.

In one of the editorials, the editor has rightly expressed a concern. 'The approach of universities and autonomous educational institutions in starting new programmes with complete disregard for academic considerations, merits serious attention. While the editor has expressed this opinion discussing about a particular programme, the above statement of the editor is true for other programmes also. For this situation the VC alone is not responsible, but the above factors too.

As I mentioned above, chaos is likely to increase, but that should not deter us from contributing our bit for the sake of posterity. In view of the above and related background, I have from the columns of Current Science felt the following points should be pondered over by the esteemed readers of Current Science.

1. Should education be totally left to the respective states or should we have a single national policy mandatory for all states to follow? Presently, education is in the concurrent list. Another alternative is to make at least some major matters as a national policy, leaving absolutely no loopholes for the states to circumvent.

2. Presently, a state university functions (or can function) on the basis of a random combination of rules and regulations of the UGC, of the respective state government and of its own (because it enjoys autonomy). It is high time that we decide on a specific method of functioning. A great deal of uniformity and collective vision is required — if not throughout the country — at least within a state.

3. How much autonomy should a university enjoy? A VC is able to create many problems in a university because of this autonomy. The same autonomy can be used by another VC to improve the university. But in the present state of affairs, I feel the extent of autonomy should be decided keeping in view the former situation.

4. It is high time that the UGC is split into CGC (College Grants Commission) and UGC (University Grants Commission).

5. The nation should ensure spread of education fairly uniformly throughout the country, obviating the regional differences present.

6. People should be educated as to why they should be serious in matters of education and S&T. People express awe at the might of the West. Similarly, people express awe when Cambridge or MIT claims a number of Nobel Prizes. It is not just the defence capabilities, but also the well-being and harmony of a society that is dependent on excellence in many branches of knowledge and spheres of human activity.

7. A long time ago, an advertisement in *Nature* for a senior academic position said 'The candidate would be judged for his quality of mind, intellect and character. I do not know

how they have judged the above, but it is worthwhile that we too ponder on these lines. Is it possible to get a person who excels in all the above qualities, for every university in the country, that too every 3-5 years? In the West, I understand that many good academicians shun not only a VC's post but even a chairman's post (Head of the Department). But in our country many are restless to rise to the above posts. Why? There is 'something' in these posts in our country which must be analysed.

References

1. Virk, H. S., Curr. Sci., 2001, 81, 628-629.
2. Basa, D. K., Curr. Sci., 2001, 80, 1364.
3. Kulkarni, S. K., Free Press J., 31 January 2001.
4. Balaram, P., Curr. Sci., 1999, 76, 859–860.

Published: *Current Science*, Vol. 81, No. 11, 10 December 2001

16

In Defence of the Vice Chancellors

A.S. Rao

Vice Chancellors (VCs) and politicians are often blamed for the condition of universities'. In reality, persons surrounding a VC are more culpable than the VC himself. Unfortunately a group of individuals (within the campus they may belong to any group or sub-group) often surround the VC and influence both major and minor academic and administrative matters, and make every VC more controversial than what he really may be.

A VC may be changed every three-four years but faculty, both academic and administrative, remain in the campus for 25-40 years. By the time they retire, the faculty may have successfully handled (read misguided) 8-10 VCs, besides more at other levels of hierarchy. Subsequently, their protégés continue.

To expect a VC who is a combination of an outstanding academician, able administrator working with selfless dedication, high integrity, excellent PR, etc., for every university in the country and that too every three-four years is impossible. Hence, there is a need to clearly state the responsibilities of and make other members of the academic and administrative community accountable as well.

It is also not fair to say that only a VC is a politician or gets appointed because of a politician. The same may hold true for a clerk, lecturer, professor, etc. Once an academician-turned full-time politician was asked 'why he had left academics to join politics'? He quipped, 'because there is less politics in real politics than in academics'! How does a politician get to interfere with the matters on university? It is we academicians who rope in politicians to get everything we aspire for. I have never come across any chancellor, VC or Education Minister who has prevented a faculty from taking classes, mentoring graduate students or reading literature in his field. For every example which one may give regarding political interference, I think there will be many examples where things have happened or not happened because of our own lobbies and schisms.

So what is required? Glasnost and perestroika. Balaram has rightly posed the question, Is this the opportune moment for a major intervention by governments, state and central, and academic bodies, which might catalyse a transformation?' Yes. But first of all they must be more transparent and restructure themselves before becoming capable of catalysing a transformation in the universities.

Another suggestion by Balaram is 'Indeed, if reform and restructuring must happen, the movement for change must come from within the universities. The faculty and administrators at our universities must be active participants in defining the reform process. Rightly said. But an anecdote highlights a problem. Once a group of faculty happened to pour out their grievance before a VC. The VC immediately constituted a grievances committee' and appointed a chairman to look into the matter. The faculty again rushed back to the VC and said: 'Sir, what have you done? The members of the 'grievances committee' are the ones who are responsible for the grievances of the faculty and students, and the chairman of the committee is the one who is the most responsible.

So what is to be done? Let readers of Current Science be active participants in defining the reform process.

References

1. Tauro, P., Curr. Sci., 2008, 94, 839.
2. Balaram, P., Curr. Sci., 2008, 94, 153–154.

Published: *Current Science*, Vol. 95, No. 6, 25 September 2008

17

Feedback on the Proceedings of the Vice Chancellors of Central and State Universities

A.S. Rao

The conference had 8 thematic areas as mentioned below, discussing a wide variety of aspects and there is a need to reflect on the following points.

Thematic group-I-university and society, access, equity, engagement and outcome

1. In spite of elaborate reservation system, still there is lot of grumbling and outrage. This is because, in view of hundreds and thousands of castes within a broad social group, the benefits of reservation have been cornered only by a few communities. Further, there are serious imbalances between the states that needs to be corrected. Hence, target groups whose GER is presently very low are to be identified and given preference. After the analysis of the recent census, and the agitations for reservations by different communities in the country, people are hoping that the present reservation system would undergo considerable changes.
2. It is said that the difference between an intelligent man and a fool is who gets the information first. The scientific community-barring a few—are totally ignorant of the state of affairs in different regions and institutes and are unable

to participate in giving feedback or decision making. Particularly the flow of money is kept a secret affair. The statistics posted on the web site should be prompt and highly comprehensive—rather encyclopaedic- so that there is no need for anyone to go for RTI.

3. There should not be any drastic differences in the basic structure and supporting grants between the universities. A central instrumentation cell duly manned and a higher allocation and insistence towards the training of the students is required.

4. To ease the burden of and increase the efficiency of VC, Registrar and COE (controller of examinations) steps have been suggested by many. They are: (a) All universities affiliate only 20-50 colleges (b) All universities may remain unitary (c) If not all universities, some more number of unitary universities may be created. (d) We may have only a two tier system vise Colleges and research institutes. A student may finish his UG/PG and get admitted into the research institutes as a regular Ph.D or integrated Ph.D. The existing universities can be converted into colleges or universities depending on their present status and the needs of the students.

5. Options for the colleges are: (a) they can be under Directorate of Collegiate education as now but empower the directorate to confer degrees. To limit the burden many directorates can be established. The other option is as suggested by above i.e. clustering of 20-50 colleges into a university and appoint a VC. Alternatively a bold step may be taken to make all colleges autonomous along with the power to confer degrees. Then they would be more responsible.

6. COE post is too heavy and often controversial. Thus, it can be split into two, one COE for UG and second for the PG (M.Sc. and M.Phil) and Ph.D's. Presently there is a heart burning among the university staff that they rarely become

COE's and this post is usually bagged by faculty from colleges or with college antecedents. Hence, if the affiliation system continues a third COE exclusively from the main campus for Ph.D may be appointed. This will help Ph.D students a lot in completing their Viva Voce after submission of thesis.

7. Pension system should be revived or an option may be given to the faculty as to which system he wants to choose, pension or matching grants system. Further, irrespective of the length of the service put in, 50 per cent of the last drawn pay should be given as a pension.
8. The way a conference of VC's has been conducted, a conference of Directors of all research institutes under all organisations be organised by the Ministry of science and Technology, MHRD and other relevant ministries and the concerned research organisations and take a stock of the situation.

Thematic group-II-content and quality

9. Following a credit based system needs a fundamental change in the question paper pattern to enable the potential students to secure the maximum grades. Guide lines should be accordingly given. While agricultural universities are too familiar with the system other universities are unable to come out of the old system and thereby students get less marks and less CGPA/OGPA.
10. Not only universities and colleges even national institutes should undergo accreditation process by a suitable body.
11. Job of IQAC should be treated as a whole time job. Presently it is a part time job where randomly a faculty is given an additional charge, for a limited period of time. A person with a background of education and education technology should be appointed as permanent in charge of IQAC and similarly so with college curriculum development cells.
12. In the west and other countries they do not have such a

large number of colleges as we have. Hence, they take UG programmes in the universities. Further, we have IISER's. Hence, our universities need not be burdened with UG programmes. And some reputed institutes want to start four year bachelor degrees.

Thematic group III-Research and Innovation

13. Research is carried out in state and central universities, research institutes under ICAR, CSIR etc. and National institutes and even in the colleges. Mandate for the research should be clearly demarcated among the above categories of institutes and accordingly funded.
14. Sharing of resources may be effectively done by instructing the PI's to make available their equipment to students for their practical's and research scholars other than theirs and a report in this connection with this be submitted to the concerned funding agency.
15. Our Ph.D's should be goal oriented and there should be a continuity of work in the PI's lab till the goal is achieved. While recruiting faculty, serious planning should be there. Recruiting several faculties from the same or over lapping discipline in the same dept., is a faulty plan. There is lot of internal brain drain from universities to national institutes. Most of the fellowship holders prefer to work with national institutes which are well equipped and funded.

Thematic Group V-Internationalisation of higher education

If foreign universities began functioning in our country it is not so much the faculty from universities which will be drained, as the delegates say, but the faculty from our reputed institutes. Foreign pay packages and environment will be better. Or else NRI scientists may join these institutes. Even if good quality foreign universities do not set up in or country, these campuses will still be better than some of ours and so many prefer to go there. This would affect primarily private institutes and not Government Institutes which charge lesser fees and adopt an elaborate reservation system. If as delegates presume, foreign universities offer only those courses with commercial returns e.g., professional and technical courses, it should be welcomed rather than discouraging, because these courses presently are highly commercialised in our country. Economically it may not make much difference (cost may even be less!) to the aspiring students and they may have the advantage of equally good or even better training.

Thematic group VI- alternative modes of delivery of higher education

Combine all the correspondence courses, presently affiliated to the universities under one umbrella of ODL (open and distance learning) supervised by the respective state planning commission and education ministry, to address the social issues, gender disparities, economic problems etc. Alternative modes such as ODL and e-learning can contribute significantly towards the goal of expansion of higher education in the country.

Thematic group VII- Models of financing higher education

Why should UGC pay salaries, when appointments are not made by them or by any statutory board? UGC should pay the salaries only if the recruitment is made either by UPSC, state public service commissions, or state TRB (Teachers Recruitment Board). A state may even form a separate board URB (university recruitment board) for university appointments. Alternatively by choice and merit, candidates from the state TRB list can be appointed in the university and the rest in the colleges. It is absolutely wrong to automatically regularise the temporary faculty who have been randomly selected and hence, may be the compromised ones. They should once again compete in an open advertisement. Temporary faculty may be recruited from the waiting list of the TRB's selection and other statutory bodies mentioned above. The conference has made a utopian resolution that political and beurocratic interference in the appointments of VC, Registrar, Finance officer and Controller of examination is to be avoided! This is possible only in one way. Appoint the senior most person for all the above posts. If need be reduce the duration of the tenure and decentralise the powers to the extent possible. Even if there is no political and beurocratic interference, it is not guaranteed that a man would function well. Like the seat of Vikramaaditya on which any man would spell only justice, the seats of power are opposite to that of the seat of Vikramaaditya. Even a man of integrity and calibre may function otherwise. Hence, some inbuilt checks are to be there. It has been rightly pointed out in the conference that absence of accountability is as much detrimental to academic excellence as the loss of autonomy. But who is to evaluate the accountability and whom to be held responsible? MHRD should take the inputs of the real stake holders i.e. students and research scholars. They can give their genuine feedback only if their identity is protected. For this MHRD/UGC should have a provision on their web site and invite feedback from all the numerous institutions of every category, across the country. When such a provision is there, even faculty can air their opinions. Similarly NAAC should elicit feedback directly on their web site without insisting on identity.

Reference

1. www.ugc.ac.in/notices/proceedings_VCConf_March_25-26.pdf

Published: University Today.

D. Miscellaneous

18

Are we not Solicited and/or Contributing in Life Sciences?

A.S. Rao

Academicians from various backgrounds have analysed and assessed the magnitude and quality of India's contribution in different areas of science and technology, based on different criteria like (a) International awards and honours, (b) patents, (c) number of publications, (d) publication in high impact journals, (e) citation index, etc. Here, I suggest yet another parameter which can be a supplement to the above criteria.

Many international publications function based on invited articles. In the publishers' jargon, 'they solicit manuscripts only from those who have made original and/or substantial contribution in a given field. The How many of our scientists have such recognition?

Being in a biotechnology department, I prefer to scan the 16 volumes of Biotechnology. The total number of chapters in these volumes is 313 contributed by 547 authors. Only one article by two authors is exclusively Indian, i.e., solely by Indian authors contributing from India, with one member in the Editorial Committee. A similar exercise with Encyclopaedia of Microbiology two yielded 298 articles written by 451 authors. Only one article by a single author emanated from India. Further, I have scanned 154 volumes of Methods in Enzymology (spanning years 1955–91), though as of today there are more than 405 volumes. There were 8620 articles contributed by 13,790 authors, of which only 22 articles are from India contributed by 30 authors. As the referee pointed out, the above plight can be shared by many nations of the world, and that USA and advanced Europe being a multi- ethnic scientific community, contributions from several nationalities, including Indians might have gone into the published work directly or indirectly. However, this should not make us complacent in view of the fact that we are the third largest scientific community, and we work and publish in English.

The eight-volume series on plant Bio-Chemistry four (180 contributors) and the four-volume series on Encyclopaedia of Molecular Biology five (480 contributors) have no Indian address, though the latter has contributions by nine Indians residing abroad.

The five-volume series on Encyclopaedia of Bioprocess Technology six contributed by 375 authors, has four authors with Indian address and nine Indians contributing from abroad.

Analysis as above may be made with other sources like Encyclopaedia of Bio-chemistry, Annual Reviews series, Critical Reviews series, Nature Reviews, etc. and also in other disciplines. In conclusion, this parameter, namely number of solicited articles in reputed compendia can also serve for assessment of quality of science contribution from any country, in any field.

References

1. Rehm, H.J. and Reed, G. (eds), A Multi-volume Comprehensive Treatise – Biotechnology (Second, completely revised edition), VCH, Weinham, Vols 1–12 (including 16 volumes of subdivision).
2. Lederberg, J. (Editor-in-chief), Encyclopaedia of Microbiology (Second Edition), Academic Press, San Diego, 2000, Vols. 1–4.
3. Colowick, S. and Kaplan, N. (eds), Methods in Enzymology, Academic Press, New York.
4. Stumpf, P. K. and Conn, E. E. (Editors-in- chief), The Biochemistry of Plants – Comprehensive Treatise, Academic Press, New York, 1980–81, Vols. 1–8.
5. Creighton, T. E. (ed.), Encyclopaedia of Molecular Biology, John Wiley, New York, 1999, Vols. 1–4.
6. Flickinger, M. C. and Drew, S. W. (eds), Encyclopaedia of Bio-process Technology, John Wiley, New York, 1999, Vols. 1–5.

Published: *Current Science*, Vol. 90, No. 10, 25 May 2006, 1308.

19

Some Negative Aspects of Our Universities

A.S. Rao

In my opinion following are some:

(IIT's, IIM's, research institutes etc. cannot be categorised as regular universities. Hence, only regular universities have been taken into consideration for giving the opinions.)

1. Teacher absenteeism either in letter or spirit.
2. Teachers are relegated vis-a-vis their counterparts in research in many ways.
3. Recruitment in the departments is highly ill-planned and therefore departments consist of a randomly assorted faculty. No rigid degree qualifications requirement and screening for recruitment to a post.
4. Indiscriminate starting of course programmes and intake of students without any regard for the availability of infrastructure, funds and manpower to train the students. There are many poorly viable programs.
5. Being a country with high population universities have mushroomed (and still there is a demand for huge number of universities). Correspondingly we do not have good teachers, researchers and funds to train the students.
6. Highly interrupted power and water supply, a problem persistent since decades.

7. Funding agencies do not fund till the end of the goal and by western standards the funding is inadequate.
8. A research worker simultaneously works on different goals (each Ph.D student works on a different goal) and finally no goal is achieved.
9. Lot of money is wasted in carrying out routine confirmatory research to roll out more number of Ph.Ds for survival.
10. Teacher's freedom to operate research schemes is very limited.
11. Multiple responsibilities of a teacher and more number of holidays is leading to meagre attention to students.
12. Foundation of students is very weak because of inadequate training in schools and colleges. However, they land up in universities. Better students opt to work in research institutes but not in universities.
13. Assembled theses are increasing. That is, students take benefit of outsourcing and finish their projects without gaining any hands on experience and such projects do not contribute much to science.
14. Most of the research goals require team work which is missing or negligible. Similarly University—Industry collaboration is missing or negligible.
15. Teachers are relegated vis-a-vis their counterparts in research.
16. Recruitment in the departments is highly ill planned and therefore consists of randomly assorted faculty.
17. No rigid degree qualifications requirement for recruitment to a post.

20

Ethics and Plagiarism

A.S. Rao

The editorial "Plagiarism—A Spreading Infection" has churned my mind. I confine myself to (a) the causes of plagiarism, (b) some remedial measures and (c) editorial ethics.

One of the causes of plagiarism is that without understanding our state of affairs, we have plagiarised from the West the concept of introducing project work in M.Sc. and even B.Sc. courses.

I wish to suggest some remedial measures to fight the trend of plagiarising at many places: (a) To remove project work/ dissertation at B.Sc and M.Sc. levels, as maximum plagiarism is inevitable here, in view of lakhs of M.Sc. students who roll out every year. (b) For every funding agency to have research journals of its own (or a journal for a combination of funding agencies) and make it mandatory for every principal investigator to publish papers and project reports in the respective journals of the funding agency. Any ill reputation/low ranking of papers/reports can empower the funding authorities to stop further funding for such investigators. This can also act as a credibility check for the funding agencies. (c) For CSIR to change the present policy wherein candidates can directly get SRF without passing the JRF entrance test, as this is creating a lot of pressure to publish papers. (d) For the Indian publishers to mandatorily get the books reviewed by specialists from developed countries before publishing them, as books by Indian authors, being published in huge numbers of late, seem to involve plagiarism from foreign works. (e) Instead of condemning the students copying term papers/assignments, teachers to concentrate on conducting a suitable written and/or viva voce exam on the respective topic, to judge whether students have understood the topic well or not. (f) Part time/ external Ph.Ds should be given leave officially at least for a period of three years to work as full time researchers. Further, all Ph.D's, regular or part time, should mention in their thesis full particulars of the funding and facilities utilised for the work.

As for the editorial ethics is concerned, I wish to relate a personal experience. Once I received a communication from a private group of people in USA, which said that as high as 90 per cent of the papers are rejected and/or considerably delayed in publication, due to badly written manuscripts. So the group said that it would help authors in writing manuscripts and would forward the same to the required journal. The price for this service is US$ 50-100 per page, with additional charges for tables, diagrams, graphs, etc. Is this ethical?

Reference

1. Balaram, P, Curr. Sci., 2005, 88, 1353¬1354.

Published: *Current Science*, Vol. 89, No. 7, 10 October 2005.

21

Sydney Altman's Didactic Remarks

A.S. Rao

In the recently organised biotech show, Bangalore 2008, during 24-26 April, the remarks of Sydney Altman, the Nobel Prize winner in chemistry from Yale University, were really instructive and didactic. Altman mentioned that in the late 1990s most of the powerful ideas in basic research that have pushed companies have come from non-profit agencies like government institutes (universities, etc.) or charitable private companies. About 80-90 per cent of new ideas come from non-profit companies. In other words, ideas do not come from companies. The same is true for physics, chemistry and the biomedical field, with 70-90 per cent ideas coming from non-profit agencies. He urged the companies to invest in academic institutions. One dollar investment by the companies in the government agencies has given 1.25 dollars back to the companies and 1.50 dollars to the society as a whole. But it takes 20 years to get the technology. Therefore, we need to be patient.

Can our non-profit agencies also claim as mentioned above? Only then, can academicians live with honour and dignity in the society. Our academicians, government and apex bodies should seriously reflect on Altman's remarks with all their implications and ramifications and strive to achieve the same distinction in our universities and other non-profit organisations, as those of USA.

In the meantime, the government should work out the statistics, i.e., the returns on investment in science and technology, and make it known to the public.

Published: *Current Science*, Vol. 96, No. 2, 25 January 2009

22

Need for Excellent Institutes, Multi-disciplinary Ph.Ds and Useful Discoveries in India

A.S. Rao

The editorial 'The mirage of world class institutions' is didactic and highly reflective. Balaram raises some pertinent questions, offers some useful comments and suggests steps to create world-class institutes. In this context, I quote Morton Schapiro, President of the North-western University, USA: 'you cannot create a world class university overnight'. According to him, combining access with affordability and ensuring high-quality undergraduate education are vital for building such an institution.

In India, there has been a tremendous expansion in education with 540-plus universities and 26,000 colleges. But this number is supposed to cater to only 12 per cent of the eligible candidates. According to Kapil Sibal* (Minister of Human Resource Development and Minister of Communications and Information Technology), we require 1500 universities and 40,000-45,000 colleges. Even then we fall short when compared to the enrollment in Western countries. At present, a large number of capable students are unable to enter government institutes in view of their limited number and are forced to join private institute shelling out a lot of money. Though there has been progress in the quantity,

*Presently Hon'ble Smriti Irani.

the quality in institutes is variable. Hence, the government has a serious responsibility to cater to the needs of millions of aspirants through an increase in both quantity as well as quality of institutions.

India also needs more number of Ph.Ds than the present 8000-plus. It is likely that 20,000 Ph.D students will graduate every year till 2020; this is equivalent to just 1 per cent of the total number of undergraduates4. A subject-wise quantitative requirement of Ph.Ds is essential for planning — this does not exist at present. The large number of Ph.D aspirants can be harnessed to solve the numerous problems facing the country. Science alone should not be treated as a panacea for these problems and scientists should not think that science would remain unaffected in spite of these difficulties. Scientists and technologists should work in close collaboration with academicians from the arts and humanities. When so many advanced countries are worried about the number and utility of Ph.Ds and thinking of serious reforms" we cannot remain unconcerned about our Ph.D system. This exercise is a responsibility of policy makers, funding agencies and academicians.

Our academicians should strive to identify the practical problems facing the country, work on them and persevere till they are solved. John Bidwell once said that useful discoveries are different from exciting discoveries. Mark Taylor has used the expression 'practical problems' citing the example of providing clean water to a growing population. Our emphasis should be on making useful discoveries. To sum up the opinions of Bidwell and Taylor, the curriculum should focus on existing practical problems, and our teaching and research should be relevant to this curriculum.

Adequate and authentic classified information about these problems and their current status must be open to the public. Every problem needs time, capital and expertise to solve. Policy makers and funding agencies should accordingly grant funds and encourage collaborations. Performers should be provided adequate resources for the required time and greater autonomy as incentives to persevere in academics and contribute to solving problems.

These approaches can enable the development of some highly useful albeit delayed world-class institutes in the country.

Acknowledgement

I thank Prof. P. Tauro for inspiration and guidance.

References

1. Balaram, P., Curr. Sci., 2011, 100, 1601-1602.
2. Srinivasan, M. and Aravind Kumar, B., The Hindu, 28 June 2011, p. 18.
3. Nayar, A., Nature, 2011, 472, 24-26.
4. Cyranoski, D. *et al.*, Nature, 2011, 472, 276-279.
5. Taylor, M. C., Nature, 2011, 472, 261.
6. Fiske, P., Nature, 2011, 472, 381.
7. McCook, A., Nature, 2011, 472, 280-282.
8. Bidwell, R. G. S., Plant Physiology, The Macmillan Biology Series, Collier MacMillan Ltd, USA, 1979, 2nd edn.

Published: *Current Science*, Vol. 101, No. 9, 10 November 2011.

23

Why not Emeritus Fellowships Exclusively for Teaching?

A.S. Rao

There is so much of concern expressed in several fora about the shortage of teachers, particularly experienced teachers. But no emeritus fellowship—who constitute the most experienced teachers—is given exclusively for teaching. Every emeritus fellowship demands a research project to be taken up during the tenure. When we badly require people to go to classes and teach, why this mandatory requirement of research for the grant of an emeritus fellowship? Experienced teachers can better serve as counsellors for students. In addition, they can also give suggestions in view of their experience to research scholars in the department and even help them in writing their thesis. This is a full-time job. Hence, there must be some emeritus fellowships exclusively for teaching.

Published: *Current Science*, Vol. 103, No. 1, 10 July 2012.

24

Some Suggestions to the Funding Agencies

A.S. Rao

To utilise national resources more judiciously and productively, each funding agency should possess the entire database of every other funding agency and function accordingly. They should take steps to avoid duplication of research projects, and institutional and regional imbalances. They should be in a position to judge whether the output of individuals/institutions is commensurate with the total funding which they have received. Funding agencies should have adequate stipulations to ensure due outcome of the project without harming the mandatory activities in the universities. Some stipulations which they can think of are officially delinking the Principal Investigator (PI)—particularly with huge grants — from teaching and administrative responsibilities till the projects are completed, providing temporary additional faculty to compensate for the PI's preoccupation with the projects, ensuring physical presence of the PI in the laboratory at least for two-thirds of the total tenure of the project, making accountable various levels of hierarchy in the institution regarding the usage and maintenance of equipment, deputing responsible persons periodically to inspect the PI's laboratory in terms of its assets and their usage, and interact with the workers about the manner and progress of the work being carried out. It is not possible for a university to keep pace with the office, laboratory and residential space requirements of every faculty member and other workers employed in the projects. Hence, funding agencies should grant some money for this along with the projects. Funding agencies should seriously ponder over the fact that most projects are wound up without accomplishing the goals because of insufficient capital, expertise and time. Funding agencies may have as much uniformity as possible in their procedures like number of copies to be submitted, mode of selection of workers in the project, manner of utilisation of grants under different categories, etc. Further, the practice of accepting advanced copies online or hard copies without the knowledge of any level of hierarchy in the host institute, must be done away with. Last, but not the least, every funding agency should post on its website all details since its inception.

Published: *Current Science*, Vol. 94, No. 11, 10 June 2008.

25

Clinical Trials in India

A.S. Rao

This is with reference to the News item 'India, ideal destination for clinical trials. The above title is apt for Western multinationals rather than for Indian/Third World citizens, as it does not reflect caution, though the text mentions some precautions to be taken. As clinical trials are a serious issue, views need to be stated point-blank. A more apt title should have been 'India being targeted as an ideal destination for clinical trials — Beware'.

I wish to slightly restate the words of the author. Since India and other developing/ under-developed countries have a plethora of poor and uneducated people, multinational companies are targeting these countries for conducting clinical trials of news drugs. Further, in these countries, regulatory laws and monitoring also are minimal weak and corruption is high, which makes them ideal for clinical trials. Conscientious people in these countries and some international NGOs have been emphasising that people in the Third World countries are used as guinea pigs for such experiments! In a country like India where there is rampant organ trade due to poverty, multinationals are lured to conduct their clinical trials. I remember reading an article on child prostitution in Bangladesh. Many children are given steroids to accelerate their growth, so that they can enter the profession early and easily. Such a thing cannot happen without the involvement of drug companies/ medical practitioners, apart from the Government's apathy. We really do not know how many such trials are being conducted on different target groups in Third World countries. I find some keywords missing in text, for example, rDNA products as drugs, gene therapy, and 'informed consent'. I wish to emphasise on the mandatory requirement of `informed consent'. A patient and his/her family members are due to be adequately and authentically appraised of the clinical trials to be conducted. This is all the more difficult in the case of uneducated people, children and mentally-challenged people. I wonder whether the Confederation of Indian Industry, while conducting its study, has bothered (a) to clarify whether there has been 'informed consent' as above; (b) to know how many trials have proved fatal. Is there timely and adequate compensation in such cases to the patient and/or his/her family members? (c) to check whether the patient and his/her family receive adequate remuneration during the trial period and for a reasonable time duration after the trial period. In the process of receiving medical assistance, outsourcing revenue and promotion of medical research, we should follow `bioethics' and not play havoc with poor, uneducated and otherwise helpless people.

Reference

1. De, Minakshi, Curr. Sci., 2005, 89, 597.

Published: *Current Science*, Vol. 89, No. 10, 25 November 2005.

26

Accommodate Waitlisted Candidates from NET Exams

A.S. Rao

There are a large number of candidates who appear for different All India Net exams for fellowships but are not able pass the tests successfully. I presume the names of the candidates who could not make it are maintained in the waiting list. Several funding agencies are at present appointing candidates who have not appeared for any All India Net exam as JRFs, project assistants, associates, etc. in various research schemes. Instead of making the above appointments a local affair I am of the opinion that waiting list candidates from the All India Net exams may be called for and selected for the various positions available.

Published: *Current Science*, Vol. 94, No. 2, 25 January 2008.

27

Biotechnology: What's in a Name

A.S. Rao

Who is a biotechnologist?—While for example every department of chemistry or physics in the country is headed by people who are formally qualified in their respective subjects, i.e., M.Sc. (chemistry or physics) and Ph.D (chemistry or physics), no department of biotechnology in this country is headed by a person who has formal qualifications in biotechnology. Not just the leader, even the rest of the faculty do not possess formal qualifications even at M.Sc. level, though we had been rolling out M.Sc. (Biotech) students since 1987. The leaders and the faculty of the biotechnology departments in this country come from an incredibly large number of backgrounds. (I wonder whether those with biotechnology degrees would one day head other science departments.) Can this randomly assorted faculty deliver the goods?

In a medical college, the MBBS programme has so many subjects: anatomy medicine to phthalmology, etc. These subjects are taught by persons who have relevant quantifications in their respective subjects. Imagine a situation, when a single person teaches all the above subjects and evaluating the candidate. Is it not the situation in biotechnology departments in the country? (A typical M.Sc. (Biotech) programme consists of courses drawn from several major disciplines. Some of these disciplines even have full-fledged two-year M.Sc. program. I do -not know how an M.Sc. (Biotech), compares vis-a-vis these students in these disciplines).

When biotechnology has been projected as something to change' the destiny of the nations is it not necessary to ensure the desirable number and kind of faculty and, of course, the funding, to ensure biotechnology teaching and research programmes, of the desired quality? As mentioned above, the faculty constitutes a random assortment from a large number of backgrounds and their number also varies from one biotechnology department to another" And the variation in the amount of money spent on a biotechnology student and research programmes is tremendous, at several places in the country.

Moreover what is the relevance of biotechnology departments, if the number of 'biotechnologists' outside the biotechnology departments far outnumbers those within? As my observation goes, for every one faculty member in a biotechnology department. We have anywhere from 5 to 100 biotechnologists outside the biotechnology department, in the same institute! So, what is the relevance of a biotechnology department with so many fierce clarinets from outside? Would it not be better if we bring them all together under one roof? (But, their number is so large that we may have to start separate institute universities of biotechnology to accommodate them).

In my opinion (a safe bet), India has the largest number of biotechnologists in the world. That is precisely the reason—why, in spite of the immense importance attached to 'biotechnology', we don't have an Association of Biotechnologist's of India, the way we have SBC(I), AMI, etc. Can one imagine the Association of Biotechnologists of India, in case it is started? It would be like an Indian electorate. Electoral arithmetic and vote banks will be its keywords. There would be an immense diversity of groups: botanists/zoologists/physiologists/Biochemists/geneticists/ morphologist-/taxonomists etc. turned biotechnologists. We have dry weight (read biomass) estimators, enzyme estimators, effectors (those who see the effect of so many things on so many things)— leaf area and root length measurers etc. Of course, gel runners, ELISA readers. callus formers (I mean up to callus formation only) organogenesisers (thanks to Murashige and Skoog). *In vitro* fertilisers embryo transfers, etc. Lastly 1 but not the least, gene cloners could sequencers (don't ask how many genes have been cloned and how many kilobase pairs of DNA have been sequenced till now and how this compares with the rate of gene Cloning and sequencing elsewhere in the world). It is simply impossible to list out all the functions. One can imagine the functioning of this association.-

Why are there this large-scale conversion and/or exodus of people (by all means) into biotechnology? Why is there an irresistible urge to use the prefix 'Bio' and the suffix 'Biotechnology' with every term/title?

It is really puzzling to students and staff alike that [he contents of so many theses, research papers and other publications" conferences, seminars, etc. and research projects funded by different agencies, are the same, as it was once upon a time but for the prefix Bio and the suffix Biotechnology to their titles.

It is worth noting that even for the work carried out on modem lines, some prefer to use the above prefix and suffix while others do not And, some even prefer to publish under the domain of -old parent disciplines, like physiology, biochemistry, genetics, microbiology etc. thought their work employs all the modem techniques. On the contrary, we have people. Even if they run a gel once, they feel badly offended, if they are addressed as anything other than as a 'biotechnologist'.

Why don't we (or don't we want to) discriminate between 'a technique' and a discipline or a branch of knowledge?

For example, ELISA is used by many researchers, plant physiologists, plant breeders, etc. Because of using this technique, they do not become qualified immunologists. Radioactive techniques find use in so many disciplines. Just because somebody has used ^{14}Cin his experiments, he/she does not become a nuclear physicist.

From time to time new techniques keep on emerging, which can be made use of by many in their respective disciplines and to solve research problems I do not know because of a new technique(s) why the system should allow one to destroy other professions and programmes to the ultimate detriment of the education system as a whole?

Published: *Current Science*. Vol. 10. No. 11. 10 June 1996.

28

When do we Learn to Properly Advertise a Post?

A.S. Rao

How well qualifications and job specifications are mentioned for a post in Nature and Science? For positions involving teaching, candidates are asked to submit a detailed teaching statement and philosophy, from their past services and for the future. The theory and laboratory courses to be taught and developed at various levels, viz. UG, PG, majors, non-majors, etc. semester-wise are clearly stated. Candidates are asked to mention their career objectives. On the research side the expertise required, areas to be developed, approaches to be used, technical and instrumentation skills required, goals to be accomplished, involvement of UG and graduate students in the research programmes, etc. are clearly stated. Further, even attitudinal requirements like unflappable temperament, impeccable interpersonal skills, commitment to UG teaching, quality of mind, etc. are mentioned. The responsibilities of the candidates and division of time and labour towards various activities like actual bench work to be done, teaching of courses, supervision, etc. are indicated. Another important component of foreign advertisements is that they also mention, right in the advertisement, what the institute is going to offer to the selected candidate in terms of office and laboratory space, equipment, start-up funds, annual operating budget, personal administrative support, etc. In striking contrast are advertisements in our media, which are too flexible. As a result, candidates from a wide variety of backgrounds stake a claim. It is high time that apex bodies give necessary instructions to universities, etc. to advertise posts with clear-cut requirements.

Published: *Current Science*, Vol. 96, No. 4, 25 February 2009.

Evaluating Scientists and 'Impact Factor'

What was the impact factor of journals in which findings of green revolution, white revolution, pink revolution, etc., were published? Further, in the present times rightly, there is an increased demand to publish research in open access journals now if all research work is published in the open access journals which are freely available, the impact factor of all re-search work would go sky high making this parameter absurd. It is therefore time to reexamine the value of the 'impact factor' and develop criteria to evaluate scientists based on their abilities and enterprise and not on the 'impact factor'.

P. Tauro[1]*
A.S. Rao[2]

1. Mangalore Biotech Laboratory, Mangalore 575 002, India
2. Bharathidasan University, Tiruchirappalli 620 024, India
*e-mail: ptauro@rediffmail.com

Current Science, Vol. 107, No. 9, 10 November 2014

Why Not All Research Data be on Open Access?

Recently DST/DBT has come out with a Draft Policy for making the research data to be on open access[1]. It is a welcome move and should move the international community towards this policy.

It is a well-known fact that publishing research work is expensive both for the investigator as well as publisher. But what is not realised is that most of the research concocted is done with support from the taxpayer but he does not get a chance to see the work published without paying. The winner in this game is the publisher who uses the copy right to make money. This is rather unfortunate and not correct when all cost of doing research including the processing cost of the manuscript, is paid through the tax payers money. In US, some universities have now asked their scientists to publish there work only in open access journals and have also asked their libraries no to subscribe to journals which are not on open access. It is time now that all countries do this since the tax payer/reader has already paid for the work through taxes and has been cheated for long.

P. Tauro[1]

A. S. Rao[2]

1. http//spicyip.com/2014/07/spicyiip-tidbit-indias-dbt-and-dst-call-for-comments-on-drafts-open-access-policy-with-respect-to-public-funded-research.html

Current Science, Vol. 107, No. 7, 10 October 2014

Index